Irene,

You've been such a great friend! I love your motivation and the way you strive to succeed in life. You are truly a great, compassionate person! I will miss all of our tutoring sessions as well as "chat sessions". I will keep our memories forever, and I wish you only the best!

Love,
Lindsay

Graduating
INTO LIFE

Graduating
INTO LIFE

THE NEXT STEPS TO MAKING
YOUR HOPES AND DREAMS COME TRUE

JOE MCGLOIN

Illustrated by Don Baumgart

INSPIRATIONAL PRESS
NEW YORK

This book is affectionately dedicated to you, the young …
May you never grow old, except in wisdom and grace.

First Inspirational Press edition published in 1999.

Inspirational Press
A division of BBS Publishing Corporation
386 Park Avenue South
New York, NY 10016

Inspirational Press is a registered trademark of BBS Publishing Corporation.

Published by arrangement with Baker Book House Company,
P. O. Box 6287, Grand Rapids, Michigan 49516-6287.

Library of Congress Catalog Card Number: 98-75430

ISBN: 0-88486-241-0

Printed in the United States of America.

Contents

Preface

There are three types of people in this world:

those who *make* things happen;
those who *watch* things happen, and
those who ask "Wot hoppend?"

You'll probably be all three of those at one time or another. But over the long haul and as a general attitude, you ought to be better than Numbers Two and Three. You ought to aim at being Number One, a leader, or at least be an active, enthusiastic companion or follower, not just watching or wondering, but helping. (That will suppose, of course, that you're smart enough to be following the right leader, not some klutz going in the wrong direction.)

Your life is a series of choices that nobody can make for you as time goes on. This book's purpose is not to make those choices for you, but to give you a few ideas that might help you to choose and to choose rightly. It's a book to help you to live as a whole person because of those choices, a person you can be proud of.

Maybe you're not big on reading and will want to drop this book about now and go back to staring at the boob tube. But if you do, you'll be missing something. I promise. If you read on, you might just learn something, or at least confirm what you already know. But even if the book were only to start you thinking about one possibly helpful idea, it would be worth your time.

So at least check out the illustrations....

"There are those who *make* things happen, those who *watch* things happen, and those who ask, *"Wot hoppend?"*

PART ONE

I'm Glad I'm Me

1

I Gotta Be Me—
I Wanna Be Me!

Sherm the Sheep

Sherm was one confused sheep—mainly because he wasn't sure he *was* a sheep. He'd grown up with two dogs at a junior-high boarding school. But suddenly the school had been closed, and Sherm had been shipped away from his dog friends to join a flock of sheep in Nevada. The other sheep weren't sure he was one of them either, so they mostly ignored him.

For one thing, Sherm liked to chase cars, which wasn't at all sheeplike. His voice disturbed them, too—he just didn't sound like they did. His attempts at "baa" usually came out more like a hoarse "arf," and now and then his voice would crack into something like "ba-yipe." The other sheep didn't exactly ridicule him, at least not to his face (that would have been un-sheeplike, too), but they made it clear they didn't want much to do with him. And Sherm honestly and sadly felt he couldn't really blame them, since, as a sheep he just wasn't with it. Especially when he compared himself with the most popular sheep in the flock, like Bucky and Mamie.

One night the shepherds had gone over to a little town they sometimes visited. It was a quiet, moonlit night, but Sherm was off by himself as usual, lonesome and down in the dumps—also as usual. Suddenly his ears perked up as he sensed something non-sheep in the neighborhood, and it was getting closer. (That was another of his peculiarities—he smelled and heard things long before the other sheep did.) Soon, though, the others also sensed the alien presence and started to fidget as two shadowy figures emerged from the darkness. As they crept closer in the moonlight, Sherm recognized them as two men who showed up only when the shepherds were gone. He remembered, too, that each time they came, one or two sheep would disappear, never to be seen again. So he sensed danger.

By now all the sheep were bleating, and Sherm started to bleat along. But, as usual, it didn't come out like a "baa" and he was surprised to see the two men glance in his direction, then hesitate, almost as though they were scared of something. He ran between them and the flock, nervously making his own strange sounds. And then, in his fright and desperation, Sherm's voice came out with a loud, strange sound that not even he had ever heard before. The two men looked at each other, then stared at Sherm in the moonlight. And then they turned and ran.

"Man," Mamie said later, when all the sheep were standing around admiring Sherm, "where did you learn to curl your lip and snarl like that? Those guys thought you were a dog, a big, strong—and mad—dog!

"Hey, Sherm," Bucky asked, "you think you could teach me that?"

"Well, I don't know," Sherm told him, his chest swelling

with pride—actually, more with joy at finally being accepted. "I don't know. It took years of practice."

Okay, he often thought later, so I'm not great at the "baa" thing, and I like to chase cars instead of just munching grass all the time. But I *can* snarl, and it did come in handy. There were still times when he wished he could do a better "baa," but the other sheep seemed to wish they could bark and snarl and curl their lip, so. . . what's the difference!

Why Do I Wanna Be Me?

Most of us waste a lot of time wishing we were as "good" as the other sheep. We'd like to be better looking, taller, and a basketball star instead of short and not even able to make the "Midgets" team; Miss America instead of Miss Backwoods; the most popular kid in the class instead of the most unnoticed; the class leader instead of, at best, lower middle. We wish we didn't have to work so hard just to reach mediocre in *any* field.

And you know what's funny? The star athlete sometimes wishes he or she were the top pupil, the class leader would like to be the star athlete, Miss America wishes she had Miss Backwoods' neat sense of humor, and so on. . . .

Well, all of us wish we had something we haven't, not really valuing enough what we do have. Each one of us, in fact, would like to have it all. But all this wishing is only a waste of time, sometimes a rather large chunk of our life—because we can't change most of those things anyhow.

Above all, though, it wouldn't be a good idea if we could!

Some Seem More Equal Than Others

The Declaration of Independence does say that we are all "created equal," but this has to be rightly understood. We're all supposed to have equal rights (which also means duties) and opportunities. That's the way our country is meant to operate, and this isn't the place to go into whether or not it always really does so.

The truth is that we are *not* "equal" in all the other ways. We're more accurately described in George Orwell's observation in *Animal Farm*: "All animals are equal, but some animals are more equal than others."

Each of us is, in fact, different from all the others—unique—all the way from our fingerprints through every part of our personality and abilities and limitations. We're supposed to be that way, and what a boring world it would be if we were all the same! *There never has been, nor will there ever be again, another "you."* Never before in history have you happened! And once you've "passed this way," never again will you either pass this way again or be repeated. You really do go around only once.

Maybe you don't stand out (and never will) as a scholar, an athlete, or a beauty queen. Well, on the other hand, maybe you do, or will sometime. In any case, you can be *you*, bringing to this world the unique things only you and nobody else can. No one but you can possibly do things *as* you. Even the kind of friendship you have to offer is unique, and no one else can be a friend in exactly the way you can. They'd be nuts to try, just as you wouldn't be playing with a full deck if you tried to imitate somebody else's unique brand of friendship.

No matter what you may think of how good or bad you are, no matter how unimportant you may sometimes feel, you are unique, and so you bring something unique to this world and to mankind. So does everyone else, each in his or her own unique way.

Above all, you always have to remember that the Lord made *you*, this unique, never-to-be-repeated individual. And so he forever loves you, not the imagined person you may wish to be, but *you*, just as you are.

Getting to Know Me

The practical thing, then, is to live, not daydream, to come to know yourself honestly, not waste your life envying others or dreaming of being someone else.

This getting-to-know-yourself bit shouldn't be a life's work, nor even close to a full-time job during any period of your life. The guy forty-five years old who says, "I just found the real me last week," sounds like he's wasted about forty years. Anyone totally occupied with trying to find "the real me" is missing everything else, and well on his way to becoming completely self-centered and selfish. Maybe even flaky.

No, you come to know yourself as you go along and as life unfolds, in action and in your dealing with others, *all* others. Just be sure to take an occasional pause to give your whole attention to asking, "What things *do* I have to work with, and how can I best use them?" Forget that stuff about "What *don't* I have, but wish I had?"

If you're not able to become a great athlete, you might

become a good photographer. If you can't dance like a pro, maybe you can converse like a warm human being. If you're not a great brain, maybe you can be a pretty fair comic. If you can't beat up on anybody, maybe you can "persuade" him or her with a brand of kindness no bully could ever even understand. If you're not the life-of-the-party type, maybe you can make the shy girl or guy at that party feel comfortable. You probably understand shyness better than does the playboy or playgirl, who generally can't be bothered with quiet types. If the class star (in brain or body or whatever) doesn't seem to want much to do with you, move on to the lesser lights who may need your friendship. You will probably discover you need theirs!

If you can't "baa" very well, maybe you can come up with a passable snarl! Or vice versa. Of course, maybe there's nothing you can do "best." On the other hand, maybe you do a number of things fairly well. Or almost fairly well. Or at least you're willing to run the risk of failure by trying. If you can't win any one event in life's Olympics, you might do pretty well in the decathlon. And maybe you're big enough to help some of the other "competitors," those back in the crowd.

Keep something else in mind, too. Stars may help, but teams do the winning. Even teams that lose on the scoreboard can win in more important ways—like in the way they lose and in the support and help the members give each other, in victory *and* "defeat."

Getting to *Like* Me . . .

As you come to know yourself, you'll see more and more clearly the gifts and talents you've been given. As you discover that you're not only unique but valuable, you'll acquire the self-esteem and sense of human dignity that is rightfully and honestly yours. Esteeming yourself for what you are isn't false pride. It's honesty. Not to esteem yourself would be dishonest, and ungrateful to the God who created you. Such esteem doesn't mean, of course, that you remain satisfied with some of your qualities that need adjustment or developing. You're always on the lookout for ways you can improve, ways of developing, growing, and maturing. You will recognize both the challenges and your capabilities and be willing to put the two together for action—to "master the possibilities."

With that kind of attitude, you'll come to know where you are and where you're going. You won't expect the miracle of instant success, but you hang on to the attitude of "I'll do what I can over the long haul." You'll learn, like a good tennis player, that you don't usually win a point with one super shot, but you have to think ahead and set up the shots in sequence. You have to be willing to take many steps to achieve a goal instead of giving up when you can't immediately hack it in one move.

Being a realist, you'll know that no matter what you do, in ten years you will be ten years older than today. It will be good then to be able to look back proudly at ten profitable, developing years instead of regretting ten years blown on wishful thinking and other trifles.

You're not just waiting in the wings now for your living to start. You *are* living right now—unless, of course, you have chosen only to dream. You can't wait until you have grown completely and become an "adult." You live *as* you grow, and you either grow all your life or you wither and die. You're already wasting time and part of your life if you only dream of winning a fortune somewhere down the road. Instead, take the first of many steps *right now* to achieve whatever your unique "fortune" is to be.

And all along the line, starting now, you'll need the guts (sometimes referred to as "maturity") to be willing to risk failure and embarrassment, and to get up and start over when you do stumble.

So...?

As you make all these discoveries about yourself, you'll see—maybe only very, very gradually—that the really "human" person will try to help others along the way to do the same.

Just as you discover positive qualities in your own personhood, you'll be apt to look for them in others, helping them to develop instead of getting discouraged, as maybe you once did, by negatives.

And *that's* exciting!

2

Maturity's Inside

The Star and the Walk-On

Ron had it all—the size and strength and speed, the jump-shot and sky-hook, the game smarts, and the desire. He spent hours perfecting his game. And it paid off. He was the University of Council Bluffs' top high-school recruit, getting a full athletic scholarship. Plus hints at lots of other fringe benefits.

Jim had never had time to play varsity basketball during his high-school years. He'd had to work too hard to get there—and to stay there. He'd played on the streets, though, whenever he got the chance, and he was good. Not great like Ron, just good. Unlike Ron, who seemed to learn everything without much effort, Jim worked hard at his studies. And that paid off in its way, as he managed to get an academic scholarship to the same university. He did love basketball, though, and with his outside work load somewhat relieved now, he thought he'd go out for basketball. So he was a "walk-on,"

and the coach gave him a chance to join the team's practice
sessions.

Jim almost quit right at the beginning, when he first saw
Ron in action—fluid motion, great shots and speed and stam-
ina, incredible ball handling, perfection. A Larry Bird in the
making. Jim stuck it out, though, even though his discouragement was doubled when the coach apparently began to
consider him and Ron for the same position, point-guard.
"So what," Jim shrugged. "What if I don't get to be a starter?
I'll probably get *some* playing time anyhow."

As the opening game of the season came closer and closer,
it became more obvious every day that Ron was sure to be the
starting point-guard. He was perfect. Well, not quite.... It
didn't seem like any big deal when Ron got called for a
technical in the first game. That could happen to anybody.
And it was only natural for him to be steamed as he sat on the
bench and watched Jim in action.

The next game, though, Ron seemed to tighten up a tad

more, and he kicked the ball into the stands when he missed an easy jump-shot. Bench again. The game after that he threw the ball at a teammate who'd thrown him a pass that wasn't quite on target.

Then, to Jim's (and everybody else's) surprise, Ron suddenly quit the team. That was an even bigger surprise than his dropping out of school later.

"I don't understand it," Jim told the coach one day. "He has it all. I don't see why he quit."

"He didn't quit," the coach said quietly, shaking his head. "I cut him."

"You cut Ron? But why? He's the best player his age I've ever seen. He could play in the pros right now."

"Maybe. Maybe not. But he can't play here. You see, Jim," the coach went on, "there's one thing Ron does *not* have, not yet anyhow. Maturity. Control. And without that. . . ." He shrugged, apparently figuring that had cleared it all up.

"Maturity? Why Coach, the guy is strong as a bull. He's smart. He gets around. The girls like him. I don't get it. He sure looks mature to me."

"Size and strength aren't enough," the coach answered. "Not even being real smart. He's a perfectionist, Jim—he blows his stack when he comes up a bit short. Until he gets those emotions under control, he won't be any great basketball player. Or anything else."

No Maturity, No Security

The coach was right—without maturity you can't get anywhere worthwhile. You might be the smartest one in the class, or the best athlete, or the most beautiful—or even all of the above. You might act cool, like you have it all, and all under control. You might *look* mature. But unless you really are mature, or matur-*ing* inside, sooner or later life will whip you. The Rons have hope of maturing, of course, as time goes by. But some make it, some don't. And those "don'ts" are easy to recognize—no matter how old they get. The immature person will be basically self-centered, with an inner attitude of "What's in it for me?" and little or no thought of what "it" might do to others. His (or her) friends are really only his servants, maybe just his flatterers. In any case they are limited to those who make him feel good, one way or another. She may smoke or drink (or probably both), not because she really likes it, but to show she's a "real grown-up woman." A guy may use his body for bullying, and a gal may specialize in tongue lashing others. The immature person will be an "escape artist," always finding a way to walk around hurdles or to substitute fun for obligation. This ID is the reason a good shrink can identify the potential alcoholic or the junkie long before he or she ever gets hopelessly hooked on dope or booze. For the young escapist, booze and/or dope will sooner or later become the way out of facing up to anything.

In a word, the immature person is self-centered. He or she wants to be the sun around which the rest of the universe revolves. The immature person is like Ron, who can't face the reality that every "sun" casts some shadows.

What *Is* this "Maturity"?

Since human types have a lot in common with animals, and even plants, to some extent we share with them the meaning of "maturity." A watermelon is mature when it is ripe. A plant is mature (to get technical, and stuffy about it) when it can take in nourishment, grow, and reproduce its own kind. The plant cycle goes from seed to green to mature to dead.

Applied to non-human animals, "maturity" takes on a much wider meaning. A puppy has to grow into maturity, and some take longer than others or never really make it at all (just like some human types). If a pup is lucky enough to have a loving human companion, it can grow up into a mature, well-mannered (well, that's part of being mature), and loving animal. Actually, the maturity and manners and such of a pet will usually reflect the maturity and sense of its human caretaker. A dog's owner either takes the care and discipline to help the dog grow and mature, and to protect it along the way, or lazily avoids the responsibility with some lame excuse like "Duke has to learn to take care of himself." No decent dog deserves that variety of owner!

When we start to move up the ladder to human maturity, though, we face a still bigger step. Much bigger. But to get at just what maturity in a human being is, we had better sift through some of the various *kinds* of maturity.

We share the concept of sexual and physical maturity with plants and other animals. Sexual maturity is easy to define. It's that point at which a person is capable of begetting children—which has nothing at all in common with being capable of *raising* children. This ability to generate arrives at varying ages, and it can come unbelievably early. It sounds incredible, but there is a record of a Brazilian girl having a baby at the ripe old age of six! Obviously, in no way is mere sexual maturity the only variety that's needed for the permanent commitment of marriage, with the serious responsibilities involved. That requires adulthood, not just in age, but inside, in deep, deep maturity.

Physical maturity is a bit harder to define. It's probably that point at which one seems to reach a sort of plateau of physical well-being in size and strength. The "prime of life" you might say. This stage, too, differs widely among individuals, as some mature physically early, some later than others, often even much earlier or later than average. Physical maturity is not only a matter of reaching full growth, because even after that full physical growth, the load will often shift, strengthening and perfecting one's physical frame. The plump girl of fifteen may be the same weight at twenty-one, but she may well look a lot different. And it's not really very bright to call a chubby guy of sixteen "Fatso," because by the time he's twenty he may be able to knock your block off.

Athletes in different sports peak out at varying ages. A boxer is pretty old for the ring at thirty, and a tennis player is usually losing some steps by then, but basketball or football players may be at their best at this age. Handball and racquetball players claim that they reach their peak just before they collapse on the court.

Okay, so we share those kinds of maturity with plants and animals. Now we move way up the scale to the types of maturity unique to us human beings: intellectual, emotional and spiritual maturity.

It's hard to discover an exact point at which a person can be called intellectually mature. It would seem to be that stage at which a person, in proportion to his or her age and experience and everything else, has enough mental know-how to be capable of learning more on his own, and who realizes that learning (from both books and experience) is not only some school chore, but a lifelong process. The intellectually mature person will realize, even though it may be a gradual process, that the more he learns, the more there is to learn. And he'll know that learning is a part of the maturation of a human being.

The biggie here, though, and the kind of maturity we mean when we talk about human maturity, is emotional maturity. That's the point at which one realizes that judgments and decisions are not to be made on the basis of "I *feel*," but rather "I *know*." Basically, emotional, or human, maturity means that one uses and controls one's own emotions, rather than letting them control him—or her.

Spiritual maturity is related to both intellectual and emotional maturity. They all go together. It's the recognition of the whole picture of life, starting with life's purpose: fulfillment with and in God. The apostle Paul spelled this out for us with his usual somewhat blunt clearness:

> When I was a child, I talked like a child, I thought like a child,
> I reasoned like a child. When I became a man, I put childish

ways behind me.... I consider [all else] rubbish, that I may
gain Christ.... All of us who are mature should take this view
of things... (1 Cor. 13:11; Phil. 3:8, 15).

So...?

So how would you describe the mature human being? You
could add to this list of qualities, but it's a start. The mature
person is one who:

1. Faces total reality without trying to blot out any of it,
   including the unpleasant things that have to be faced in
   any life...
2. Is able to distinguish between means and goals, and so
   can understand that all things seen and heard and experienced are means to one's only final goal, God....
3. Has a knowledge and an emotional stability befitting
   one's actual age—using, of course, but not controlled
   by his or her emotions...

4. Has an honest sense of his or her gifts, self-worth,
   abilities...
5. Is not discouraged by his or her own shortcomings, nor
   envious of the talents of others (real or imagined), but
   keeps on working to improve even if it means having to
   get up and start over....
6. Has the courage to follow personal convictions, to be
   his or her own person, no matter what happens or who
   says otherwise....
7. Has a sense of values, knowing which things are of
   importance and which are trivia....
8. Practices the discipline of acting on that sense of
   values—for example, sometimes choosing to study
   when he or she would sooner be partying or watching
   TV....
9. *Realizes that love and sacrifice are inseparable.*

3

Little + Little = One Lifetime

Take the Heat—or Freeze

Goldie ran into Bertie at the Silver Bullet in a little town in Montana. It was love at first sight, and they soon established a relationship—a "commitment," as they liked to refer to it. But no matter what they called it, it meant that Goldie moved in with Bertie. Not many months later, though, Goldie met Ferdie at the same Silver Bullet, and she knew right away that she loved him more than Bertie. "Besides," she told her best friend, Sylli, "Bertie was a pig. He just wouldn't take a bath. His feet always stunk."

"Well," Sylli consoled her, "at least you didn't marry the bum."

"Of course not," Goldie laughed. "When you get married you have to make all kinds of promises and try to stick it out no matter what, even if their feet stink. And it's a real hassle when you have to bust it up. I'd sooner do the relationship thing—you can get out of that right away when something goes wrong. Especially now that Ferdie has come along."

Kathy, an orphan, was just about to start her second year of college when all her money ran out, and a part-time job just wouldn't cut it for her anymore. Because there was no way, either, that Kathy could handle both a full-time job and full-time college, she quit school so she could enjoy some luxuries like eating and paying the rent.

But Kathy still hung on to the determination to get back to school if and when she could. A year later, she decided to take a crack at the Peace Corps, so she signed up for a two-year hitch in Landivar, in Latin America. There she found herself with the responsibility of taking care of what seemed like countless hungry and sick people, working alongside doctors and nurses who gave up their vacations and sometimes a lot more to work with the poor. When she came back to the States, Kathy had lunch one day with Joan, one of her former classmates, and she was surprised to see how young the girl seemed, not so much in appearance as in her interests and attitude. Or maybe, Kathy thought, I just got older. Joan seemed more interested in guys and parties and TV than in the poor and sick and hungry. But after all that Kathy had experienced in the past two years, parties and such just didn't seem to be very important. Well, guys were still important, but not at the top of her list.

Kathy, now twenty-two, went back to work, this time at a hospital. There she met Tom, a doctor, and soon they were married. She kept on working until she was pregnant with Tom, Jr. Since Kathy, Jr. came along a couple of years later, Mom had her hands—and her mind—full. Along the way, she and Tom had to work out some problems and sometimes some disagreements, mainly due to his dedication to his work, which Kathy thought was so absorbing that he was neglecting his family. They did work things out, though, realizing that neither one of them was as perfect as they had imagined when the first blast of love had partially blinded them to the realities of sharing their lives. So they made it, their love deepening day by day.

But then, when Tom, Jr., was six and his sister, four, Doctor Tom, who had always overworked, died of a heart attack. So Kathy had to go back to work once more. When the kids were both in their teens and Kathy was thirty-seven, she started thinking seriously about getting back to school.

"I'd like to go back," she told Joan, who by now had a family of her own. "In fact, I wish I could be a doctor."

"So why don't you?" Joan asked. "After all, there *are* grants these days, and with your experience you'd be a cinch to get one."

"But it would take eight years," Kathy objected.

"So," her friend asked, "if you become a doctor, how old will you be in eight years?"

"You know that—forty-five."

"And," Joan went on, "if you *don't* become a doctor, how old will you be in eight years?"

"Why, forty-five, of course. Uh, oh . . .!"

So Kathy became a doctor, an outstanding doctor in fact, keeping so well up in her field, obstetrics, that she received some award or other almost every year.

Make or Break

One big giveaway to the immature is that they always try to make sure there's an escape hatch handy. Like Goldie. She hasn't the maturity—and probably never will have—to make a commitment that would bind beyond even the tiniest hassle. She claims to be "in love," and that "our love will be forever," and all those lies. But she hasn't the maturity, either—and probably never will have—to know what love really is, to recognize that love isn't only "He'll do anything for me," and that love and sacrifice—on *both* sides— are inseparable. So, like all immature people, Goldie will give up and dash for the escape hatch at the first hint of something—big or little—that might threaten her own selfish whims.

Kathy, on the other hand, managed to come up with a decent degree of maturity early in life, and she kept deepening and acting on that basic maturity all the way along, at every stage of her life and in the face of every obstacle she encountered. (The Peace Corps experience had been one giant step in maturing for her.) She understood, without ever putting it into words, that maturity is a lifelong process, that, in fact, maturing is a more accurate description than matured. Maturity, Kathy had learned, is a journey, not a terminal.

To *Keep* Maturing, You Have to *Start* Maturing

As you've probably noticed, sexual and physical maturity are automatics. You don't have to do anything to achieve them—they just happen. Of course, you can help to make yourself a better specimen by the time you reach physical maturity—by living clean, exercising regularly, and such. But you'll reach your physical peak on schedule anyhow, no matter how strong or weak that peak might turn out to be.

Human—emotional and intellectual—maturing, though, has to be largely a conscious process, one you will either cooperate with or miss out on. Since it's also a lifetime job, it either progresses or dies. That's why maturing is more accurate here than matured. "Maturing" sounds like "living" (and so it is), while "matured" sounds more like "dying," the step just before "rotting" (and so it is!).

Unlike sexual and physical maturing, we have to help along the process of maturing emotionally and intellectually. Otherwise, we fall behind schedule as human beings, or we even drop out. We have to remind ourselves, now and then at least, that some effort is needed if we're going to mature gracefully. And we pull that off by the right use and the correct proportions of everything in our lives—our fun, our study, our games, our friendships and other relationships, our work, our thoughts, our attitudes—the whole bit.

At each stage of our lives there are differing degrees of maturity, and that's just as it should be. So you can be mature, or immature, at any age. It's your choice, sometimes not an easy one in detail, but still a choice.

If you're fifteen and act fifteen, you're mature enough for your own present space. But a person who is thirty and still acts fifteen is immature. Notice, though, that the fifteen-year-old can fall into immaturity in either direction—by acting like eight or pretending to be twenty-four. Trying to act like someone twenty-four (especially by imitating only some stupid externals, such as smoking, drinking, careless driving, sexual misuse) is a stronger sign of immaturity than reverting now and then to ten-year-old acting (as long as it's only "now and then"!). You can't look at a four-year-old dressed up in a formal and believe she's mature. On the other hand, maybe the parents who dressed the kid that way are more truly immature than she.

You *allow* yourself to mature emotionally, but you also have to *help* yourself do so. The important thing is that you let no one or nothing slow you up or stop you en route. If you let your peers retard your maturing process, you lower yourself to their level of immaturity. The good news is that you're capable of handling all the peer pressure you're hit with. The bad news is that the peer-pressurers, with their threat of ridicule, are going to keep trying to hit on you all your life. To the maturing person, though, the risk of ridicule is completely unimportant when compared with life's real values, with the important goals.

Sometimes, circumstances in your life, some of them even tragedies, will push you into taking a much longer stride toward maturity. Peace Corps workers and missionaries invariably experience this, finding on their visits home that their interests and concerns show them that they've far outdistanced their peers in maturity. Like Kathy, they're sharper at spotting the difference between trifles and valuables.

Or maybe a young person will suddenly be saddled with some staggering responsibility: serious illness or death of a parent; neglect or abuse by an alcoholic father or mother; desertion of the family by either parent. From such tragedy can come the strength of maturity—*if* one accepts the situation instead of collapsing. The immature do collapse—the maturing face the circumstances and handle them.

A very important part of continuing to mature is continuing to learn, assuming that one has started the process somewhere along the line. A person cannot be humanly mature without being intelligently mature—which is also obviously a lifetime task. People who figure they have learned enough after graduating from—or just leaving—high school or college (or even worse, elementary school or junior high) are dead on the vine, unless, of course, they realize their mistake soon enough. Learning requires a lifelong curiosity, an interest in *everything*, not just in the practical know-how for making a living, but in all possible knowledge. The engineer or doctor or nurse or farmer who knows *only* his or her own field, or who fails to keep up to date in that field, is not mature. This is not a complete person, but just a machine programmed to do only one thing, over and over and over again.

The maturing person will be smart enough to take the pains to learn as he or she grows and will not be too lazy to look things up (even spelling!). Actually, continual learning is not just knowing a lot of facts, but knowing where to look for answers—then having the good sense, drive, and maturity to take the trouble to look. And if you start that early enough, it will get to be a habit.

The Choice Is *Now*

Okay, so maturity is a lifelong job. Nowhere along the line of life can anyone lean back and honestly say, "At last I'm completely mature." Even if you do mature according to your own capabilities and your own schedule, there will be lapses and relapses. A high-school senior once remarked about his sophomore sister, "I don't know what's with her— one day she acts like a woman, but the next day she's more like an eight-year-old." The problem is that *he* followed the same pattern—a man one day, a kid the next.

And that's as it should be. Part of the lifelong maturing process is being able to have the courage to take two steps forward for every step you've slid backwards. And, for the most part, to act your age—no more, no less.

If you're listening at the right time and place, you'll some-time hear the moanings of some girl who "never had much of any teenhood, with the fun and dating and stuff" of that period. Maybe it was because she had a baby when she was only in her early teens and—suddenly acquiring a sense of responsibility—said, "If I'm old enough to generate a baby, then I'm old enough to take the responsibility of raising my child." Maybe that's right, maybe wrong. Maybe she mar-ries, maybe not. But while the other kids her age are having a reasonable portion of fun in their lives, this girl is tied down by cares and responsibilities beyond her years.

So...?

You've noticed the word *act* pretty often here: "*Act* your age...*act* maturely...*act* this way, not that way...." So what does "act" mean here? What actions reflect maturity?

Unfortunately, you can't delegate anybody to answer that for you. The answers are unique for each individual. You might, however, find some general guidelines and bases for your own choices listed at the end of that previous chapter. Try it.

As you can see, there ought to be a natural and honest pride in maturing gracefully through each phase of your life. The permanently immature will never know what that pride—that human dignity—is.

But *you* will.

4

"I Am Fearfully and Wonderfully Made"

Three Persons, Three Answers

Larry Louder was going around school inviting folks to the kegger he was planning. There were, of course, some he didn't bother to ask, since he was sure they'd refuse or, if they did come, just wouldn't fit in. He took a chance, though, on some "borderline cases." This is how it went with three of them:

"Sunday afternoon," Larry told Marge. "Right after the game."

"But last time," Marge objected, "the cops busted it up. It was scary. Some of the kids got arrested. And most of us were in trouble at home for a long time. Besides, we lost a lot of money with all that beer getting thrown out."

"No sweat," Larry smiled. "That's all taken care of this time. There's this spot south of town, next to the Miller farm, way back off the road in the trees. We could hide a whole used-car lot back there."

"Well, I don't know," Marge hesitated, obviously reluctant. "I have a lot of homework to get done. . . ."

"You've got all weekend," Larry insisted. "Come on, Marge—it just wouldn't be the same without you. Everybody wants to see you there—especially Gus. You and he seem to have a thing."

"Gus will be there?"

"Yeh. And he'll sure expect you to be. Come on—what do you say?"

"Well—well, okay. I'll be there."

Larry wasn't sure about George. He was a good enough guy to be around, but he didn't seem to be around all that much, like at parties. So Larry wasn't all that surprised when George hesitated.

"I—I don't think so," George told him. "Man, I'd really like to come, though. The problem's my mom. I know she won't let me. She can really be tough that way."

"How about your old man—can't you get him on your side? Dads dig beer."

"I told you Mom is tough," George laughed. "No, Larry, sorry. They just wouldn't let me."

Okay, so scratch one, Larry shrugged.

Then he spotted Trish down the hallway. She was really a front-runner, with a sensational build. He'd never seen her at a party or much of anywhere else, but she was sure worth a try.

"A beer bust?" Trish asked. "You gotta be kidding!"

She sounds interested, Larry thought. "No way. It's for real."

"No," Trish said.

"What?" Larry couldn't believe it.

"No!" Trish repeated. "I've got a lot more important things to do than that."

"Well, okay then." *Who needs you anyway*, he thought, as he watched her walk away. . . .

Larry managed to get a good crowd together for the kegger, and, as he'd promised, the police never stumbled onto it. Some of the parents undoubtedly suspected, but by then it was too late and they didn't matter anyhow. He was already making plans for the next one.

There seemed to be more absentees than usual on Monday. There were a few walking wounded, too, even more than most Mondays. Larry fell asleep in every class, and at least one teacher had a hard time waking him. At volleyball practice, Trish wondered why Marge kept missing so many easy shots.

"Well, I'm kinda tired," Marge told her. "We had this party, you know, and it was a real blast."

"Yeh, sure, I can see that," Trish muttered, as another ball caromed off Marge's hands and both she and the ball dropped to the floor.

When You *Want* to Say No, Just *Say* It!

Marge, George, and Trish all *wanted* to say no. None of them really wanted to go to Larry's kegger. But only one did say no—Trish.

Marge hesitated, then gave in and said she'd be there, probably because she was afraid Gus would think less of her if she didn't show. She didn't really want to go, but. . . .

George wanted to say no, too. But he didn't say it—well, not directly. Instead, he came up with an alternative, "My mom won't let me." Not a bad gimmick that. After all, one job parents have is getting their kids off the hook and taking the "blame" for it themselves.

Only Trish came right out with what she meant. She said "No!" loud and clear. No hedging, no excuses, just one simple word that says it all.

So why did Marge agree to do something she didn't really want to do? And why didn't George come right out and say that he didn't want to go?

Fear. They were both scared. Chicken. (If you admire Trish for having the courage not to mince words, you have to have the guts to hear honest words, too.) They were all (Trish, too!) scared of one thing: peer pressure, what the others might think of them, a drop in popularity, being labeled "out of it." George found a way, and a good enough way, of not seeming to be "out of it" by passing the buck. Trish had the courage to let her own feelings and principles be known.

I'm My Own Person

It may well be that the toughest problem facing young people today is exactly this: peer pressure. That means being muscled into doing something one knows is wrong and really doesn't want to do anyhow. Or the pressure to skip something one knows should be done—like regular church attendance, prayer, helping others (like the shy and/or boring kid in class), or just being an open Christian in action. That pressure can be spoken or unspoken and may, in fact, originate and grow only within the mind and imagination of the victim.

The threat behind the muscle is always the same: "You're not one of the crowd unless you do this. . . . You're out of it, a nerd. . . . The kids won't want anything to do with you and won't ask you again." And the "reasoning" behind the threat is the lie that "Everybody who is anybody is doing it, so how come you want to be an oddball or a hermit?"

But there's a lot more behind it than that. Take a look inside the peer-pressurer and you find a really mixed bag. He (or she), despite the outside bluster, is weak, without the courage to stand up for what's right. The camouflage for that weakness is to try to get as many as possible acting the way he does, so he can claim, "If so many are doing this, it must be okay," or "If so many are not doing that, it must be only for oddballs." His weapon is ridicule, and if you want to characterize him in one word, he's a bully. That means he's en route to ending up like all bullies. Like so: "Aggressive children who bully and harass classmates grow up to be less successful as adults . . . unemployed or in prison. . . ." (That's from a 22-year study of 875 original third grade participants and 300 adults now 30 + years old from that group, reported in *Omaha World Herald* early in 1987.)

Peer pressure is a phony, and the dire results of the threats usually don't follow at all. What does follow from meekly knuckling under the pressure is a warped personality—and guilt and a lack of respect (from yourself *and* others). Sure, you might seem to attract a certain admiration among a few for a short time. But these probably don't form the crowd you really would like to be popular with—and, even there, a lack of respect is always lying beneath the seeming approval. This is precisely what has usually happened to delinquents. They've lost all respect for themselves, and they don't seem to get any respect from those they most want it from. They sold out respect when they believed the phony sales pitch of peer pressure. A self-image is a terrible thing to waste!

After all, if you can tell a lot about a person by his friends, you can also guess something about him from his enemies. And peer pressurers make the best enemies. At least they're certainly not friends, since a real friend seeks *good* for his friend, not building his own ego at the cost of an alleged friend's well-being.

There's been a big cliché going around for some time now: "Say no to drugs." And that's perfect advice, the only drawback being that one wonders why it took so long to be said. On the other hand, that simple, sane exercise of mature thinking and action should not be restricted only to the offer of drugs. It ought to be the answer to any sort of push in the wrong direction, like toward a misuse of sex, or booze, or whatever. A person will not mature by saying no to drugs while substituting booze or sexual activity for the stuff. Not unlike that mythical group known as Tobaccoholics Anonymous, who are said to describe their healing sessions this way: "Whenever we feel tempted to have a cigarette, we get together and get drunk instead."

Enough of the negatives, though. If I concentrate enough on the positives, the negatives have no space. And the positive is that I am a human being, an individual, unique human being, and that, as such, I'm either my own person (the positive) or I'm a phony (the negative). And that goes for all of us human types!

Now being "my own person" doesn't mean setting myself apart from the human race, nor from my peers. No way. I don't want to be excluded from the crowd. But I don't want to be only a mindless blob inseparable from that crowd either. I want to be me, and you want to be you—an individual, not a faceless "youth," not even "one of the Smith kids." I want to be recognizable as an individual person. Joe Smith or Joan Smith—"me."

If and when that crowd takes a wrong turn, I—Joe or Joan Smith—will step aside and let them go, not meekly allowing myself to be hustled along against my inner wishes. That's the difference between a person and a machine, or a bowl of Jello.

Being my own person means that nobody, but nobody, is going to make me do something I consider wrong, harmful to myself or anyone else. It means that I'm not going to be snowed by threats like "You're not my friend if you don't do this," with the implication that "Nobody else will want anything to do with you after this either." I'd sooner hang on to my own honest pride and self-esteem.

The paradox here is that, far from losing respect by puncturing the popularity-myth balloon, the independent person gains respect, often even gets envied, while the timid collaborator will rate only contempt. The threat of ridicule if one refuses to go along is usually only a threat, although it may sometimes materialize externally. But real ridicule, when one meekly gives in to peer pressure, is internal and in the mind, with all its very real opinions.

There is a genuine, admired beauty and satisfaction in being your own person, a quality that non-persons like peer-pressurers secretly envy. As a matter of fact, the person acting on principle will sometimes cause even the peer pressurer to wonder, or even to change. Eventually anyhow.

Being your own person means sticking your neck out, taking risks, no matter what you're afraid others might say. During a Chicago firefighters' strike, it was generally agreed that no alarms were to be answered. One fireman, though, despite the glares of his co-workers, rushed to the scene of a fire, raced up the stairs of the burning building, crawled through smoke without a mask until he saw two legs, and pulled an unconscious old man to safety. *His own person.*

Roger Staubach, one of the greatest quarterbacks of all time, once said that he felt that his comment—"I just don't believe you can be a full person until you've given yourself over to Christ"—was treated by some with cynicism and ridicule. "I don't wear my religion on my sleeve," he said. "But I'm not ashamed of it either. And I'm not ashamed to talk about it." *His own person.*

Heather Thomas, a senior at an Omaha high school, is, along with seventy-nine other teenagers, already in a Bible-study group at their church by six every weekday morning. It's held that early because all these kids are involved in lots of other activities the rest of the school day. "Some of the kids say I'm crazy," Heather says. But she and the others in the group (there were sixty one year, eighty the next) know that being there is vastly more important than what "they" might say. *Their own persons.*

So...?

Self-esteem and honest pride are vital if you are to live and mature as a human being. And they can't be gotten if you are a sucker for peer pressure, which means you are not your own person.

"I'm too good for that' ought to be our ready answer when pushed to do something we know is wrong or to omit what we know is right. That's another way of saying, "I refuse to be a slave to anyone or anything." Before we knew about all the physical dangers of smoking, a great man said he would never take up smoking, for one reason because it was a form of slavery. And since he loved the theater, he said he didn't want to be distracted during a play or other performance by aching for a smoke. He preferred to fully enjoy the play. You, too, ought to reject slavery and choose freedom, the freedom to do what's right, so you can fully enjoy life.

Remember this? "God created man in his own image, in the image of God he created him; male and female he created them" (Gen. 1:27). And your reaction? "For you created my inmost being.... I praise you because I am fearfully and wonderfully made..." (Ps. 139:13–14).

Aren't you too good to settle for anything less?

5

"Though a Righteous Man Falls Seven Times, He Rises Again"

The Survivors

Julius and his friend Henry were on their way home from a party. They had left early, but still they were tired. Since they knew they had to be fresh for class in the morning, Henry was pushing the car so they could get some sleep. Both were just twenty years old, and they were studying for the diplomatic corps at the university.

They were just about to their freeway exit when their car was sideswiped by a van (driven by a drunk, it was learned later). Their car hurtled over an embankment and slammed into a tree on the passenger side, leaving the car totaled and the two young men broken and unconscious. A passing motorist spotted the car, and soon the two were in the hospital. Henry's injuries were serious, but since he had been

driving, he wasn't in as bad shape as Julius, who was hover-
ing between life and death, badly smashed up.

After two or three weeks it was clear that both of them were
going to make it. But Henry had such a badly shattered leg
that he would probably limp the rest of his life. Julius was
paralyzed from the waist down, and he wasn't in anywhere
near top shape from the waist up either.

Henry got out of the hospital within a month. He had to use
crutches, but he could get around slowly. The trouble was
that more than his leg had been broken: his whole spirit was
shattered. All he seemed able to think of was "Why me?" He
didn't even seem to notice that his friend Julius was much
worse off. He didn't consider going back to school, just went
to his parents' home to live (if you could call it that). Little by
little Henry became the complete hermit, hardly ever even
venturing out of the house. The psychiatrists his father hired
didn't seem to help him at all.

At first Julius did his own share of asking "Why me?"
Time dragged on, as he spent three years in and out of
hospitals, his paralysis apparently permanent. Obviously his
hopes for a diplomatic career seemed destroyed along with
his body. Still, somewhere in the back of his mind and heart
was the desire to whip this thing. He didn't know how, or
what direction it might take, but Julius never lost hope completely, although of course, he had his highs and lows.

On one of his "down" days, Teresa, a young nurse, finally
got fed up with his sour mood. "Come on, man," she told
Julius, "you're *alive*—at least physically. Why not use
what you've got instead of griping so much about what you
don't have?"

"What I've got is half of me," Julius sulked.

"You've got your mind," she answered. "And your
hands. Some people don't."

"Big deal. So I have hands. Not much use if I can't get
anywhere with them."

Teresa shrugged in despair, then slammed out of the room, only to reappear a few minutes later with a guitar. "Here," she told him, practically throwing the guitar at him, "fool around with this for a while."

Julius didn't know anything about music, and he told Teresa so. But she only grinned, said, "So learn," and walked out the door, leaving him holding the guitar.

Julius did learn how to play the guitar. And he got out of the hospital, gradually and painfully getting back his legs. He became, in fact, a pretty fair musician, and a better-than-fair singer. In the years to come, he managed to get over three hundred gold or platinum records, becoming the top-selling pop singer in the world.

Julio Iglesias might have gone the way of Henry and stayed down. Instead, he got up and started over.

Saint: A Sinner Who Keeps Trying

Up to here we've been considering some of the items we have to have if we're to mature gracefully as human beings. But without one other ingredient, they'll all be useless. Or, more accurately, unused.

If we don't have faith and hope and courage enough *to get up and start over* as we go, and sometimes stumble, through life, it's all over. We won't mature. We won't grow. Over the long haul, we won't make it as a person.

There's no question about it—no one is going to get through life without stumbling or meeting some failures. Being human supposes being limited, imperfect, subject to making mistakes. Like two men who lived back there a couple of thousand years ago. Both were carefully chosen to handle a most important operation. Both were painstakingly trained for the task. But then both of them, under pressure, fell flat on their respective faces. Both failed miserably when the going got tough.

One of those men hung himself. The other one struggled to his feet, sought out and got the healing he needed, started over, and went on. Gloriously, in fact. Judas and Peter were both losers along the way. But Peter got up again to become a big winner.

If life hands you a lemon, make lemonade.

You can either give up or get up. When life hands you a lemon, you can either spend the rest of your life thinking of little else and muttering "Why me?" ("Why not me?" would make more sense!) or you can make some lemonade out of it. Like Henry, you can spend a lifetime brooding over your mistakes or your trials, bemoaning things you no longer have. Or, like Julio, you can take what you do have and use it to the fullest.

The truth is that you don't prove much about yourself until you are challenged. When one of his executives was praising a new employee, a shrewd employer remarked wryly, "Yes, but let's wait and see how things go when he stumbles or something goes wrong."

Stumbling, falling—either through your own fault or maybe carelessness, or getting hit with something you yourself didn't cause (like Julio's accident)—is usually not all that important. But it is inevitable. What *is* a must is that you have the courage and faith and trust and just plain guts to get up and start over again. Each time.

In pioneer film days, there was one actress who stood out over all the others: Mary Pickford. When she was asked once about the fear of failure, she said: "If you have made mistakes, there is always another chance for you. For this thing we call 'failure' is not *falling* down but, instead, giving up and *staying* down."

Okay, so you will stumble. Life is sure to have its crests and troughs. Expect them, and when you're on a crest or a high, prepare for the low; and when you're in the trough, know that the crest will come sooner or later, if you go for it. The idea is to use both situations, playing one against the other, not letting either one fool you into playing dead.

You are bound to fall short of your ambitions and ideals sometimes. You'll sometimes be a Charlie Brown, wondering how you can approach "that little red-headed girl," but never getting up the nerve to do so. Or maybe you *are* that little red-headed girl, wishing that cute Charlie Brown would speak to you. Even worse, some personalities stay more like Linus, who said he couldn't think of anything to say to that new little girl down the street, "so I hit her."

Depending on your age and stage of maturity, all those doubts are normal. So are your mistakes, even your faults. But there's one thing you have to avoid through it all: discouragement to the point of giving up. That blows the whole scene and brings you nothing but aches and pains—mental, spiritual, even physical. Discouragement has lots of relatives: the lack of self-esteem and self-confidence you must have to live rightly; self-pity (which is a close relative of egotism, the wrong kind of pride); losing sight of the goal;

trouble in concentrating on anything worthwhile or getting things done; depression; and finally despair. Maybe even suicide.

Discouragement can make you a quitter and a loser. But only if you allow it to take over your life.

Okay, so that's the negative side of it, not getting up. But there's no reason for you to stay down when you've slipped. Nothing is keeping you down. And you get up by looking at what you do have instead of at what you may have lost or never had. This is what helps so-called delinquents turn a corner, putting the falls and stumbles behind them where they belong and using the good things they've finally discovered in themselves, usually with some caring person's help. It's the same thing the physically disabled learn—looking at what they have, not at what they haven't and using every inch of it instead of wasting their time moaning in self-pity.

If you manage to get up, your self-confidence will return, even though it may come only gradually. You'll need patience with yourself, along with the work and struggle and maybe even pain. You'll need honest self-criticism, which means not exaggerating your shortcomings, but honestly and calmly facing yourself, faults and all. It means confronting yourself *constructively*, not negatively, with an eye to seeing what you can *do* about your faults by using the abilities you *do* have.

To get yourself back on the track, you'll sometimes need forgiveness and healing. From God, of course—and he's not just willing to forgive you, but eager to do so, no matter how often you need it. You may need forgiveness from another human being, too. You can even survive without that, if that person refuses to forgive. But it helps if he or she is "Christian" enough to forgive. More important than forgiveness from any other human being, though, is your forgiveness of yourself. Without that one, you'll stay right down in that rut.

But you can climb out any time you remember that "God and I can do anything." Like so:

> God, sometimes I just want to give up, stop dead in my tracks, go off some place and hide. I get so tired and don't want to try any more. Where can I find the strength to go on? The hope that things will eventually get better isn't enough. The thought that adversity builds character doesn't convince me. The only thing that gives me any hope is the example of Your Son. He didn't quit even though He faced death, which He conquered in His resurrection. May what He did teach me. May I find in His life the pattern according to which I can live mine. And may I try—at least in a small way—to urge others to keep trying even though they feel they've come up against a dead end. [This is from *A Pocketful of Prayers*, Carillon Books, St. Paul, Minn.; *Catholic Digest*, 1976; and a million other places!]

The physically disabled, being so close to that Cross of Christ, can teach us so much—like an attitude that "It isn't suffering that's the tragedy—only wasted suffering." And a frequent prayer that says, "Thank you, Lord, for all you have given me, for all you've taken away, and for all I have left."

If you are looking and listening, there will be examples everywhere: a Joni Earecson, paralyzed from the neck down, yet a consummate artist, holding the brush in her teeth. There's the great ex-Viking football player, Karl Kassulke, paralyzed in a motorcycle accident, yet now the highly respected defensive-back coach at Bethel College in St. Paul, Minnesota. There's Al Sparlis, who was an orphan and then graduated into a reformatory for a six-year "education." But not too long ago, he was inducted into the College Football Hall of Fame, having been an outstanding football star at UCLA. He also became a highly decorated war hero and an associate vice-president of Coldwell Banker, the nation's largest brokerage house. He had to get up lots of times!

The list could go on forever. In every case you'll find a
person who has fallen or been felled, but who had the faith
and human pride and know-how to get up and start over
instead of just lying there moaning. Lots of people simply
refuse to stay down, to quit.

Like Max...

Max Cleland is a triple amputee, courtesy of Vietnam. He
was President Jimmy Carter's appointee to head the Veterans'
Administration, and later on secretary of state in Georgia. At
his installation as Veterans' Administrator, Max recited this
prayer:

> I asked God for strength, that I might achieve...I was made
> weak, that I might learn humbly to obey. I asked for health,
> that I might do greater things...I was given infirmity, that I
> might do better things. I asked for riches, that I might be
> happy...I was given poverty that I might be wise. I asked for
> power, that I might have the praise of men...I was given
> weakness, that I might feel the need of God. I asked for all
> things, that I might enjoy life...I was given life, that I might
> enjoy all things. I got nothing that I asked for, but everything I
> had hoped for...Almost despite myself, my unspoken
> prayers were answered. I am, among all people, most richly
> blessed. [Anon.].

We've been discussing maturity. There it is!

Okay, what have you learned so far? First, that you *are*
valuable. Next, that to keep that value and raise it, you have
to act on principle, not just on feeling or mood. Above all,
you have to have the good sense and courage never to give
up, but to get up when you've stumbled.

You know perfectly well that you can't manage that all by
yourself. You need help. And the only consistent surefire

help will have to come from the source of life, the Lord. So, having spent some time here reading and (hopefully) thinking, mostly about yourself, now you ought to think about yourself in your relationship to God—who is always around. He is *eager*, not to do it for you, but to help, maybe to forgive and heal, and always to love.

PART TWO

God's Glad I'm Me

In the first section of this book, the subject was mainly "me"—the concept of oneself as an individual. Only in passing (but because it's impossible to fully separate "me" from God) did anything about God show up directly. But since, if one tries to separate "me" from God, all one manages to do is isolate the me, in this section we will more directly discuss me plus God, our basic relationship with and to him.

To be a perfect parent does not require perfect children. . . .

6

"We Live by Faith, Not by Sight"

Two Men

Mark was a very successful television and movie producer and director. He had it all—the success, the money, the family, homes, cars, comfort.

But then, during one short period of his life, Mark was hit with one trial after another. His wife died. Then two of his children. Mark was as strong and healthy and wealthy as ever, but he had to face one crisis after another through those he loved.

As a celebrity, anything connected with Mark was "news," so he showed up on many a talk show. On one of these appearances after the various tragedies he had experienced, the host asked, "But Mark, what's your secret? How do you manage to put up with all these tragedies, and still apparently stay calm and peaceful and go on with business as usual?"

"Well," Mark smiled, "you have to roll with the punches, no matter what. Every life has some tragedy in it, some more, some less. My work is a big help, of course—it's my whole life now."

"So your secret is 'That's life'? That's *it*?"

"That's it," Mark agreed. "But I don't think it's any 'secret' really. At least I didn't exactly coin the phrase."

A year or so later, *Time* magazine noted Mark's death, "by his own hand...."

Tom Cassidy never made *Time*. He had never come close to being wealthy or a celebrity or even a newsworthy rabble-rouser. So he was hardly a "success" or even "news" by a *Time* or Hollywood definition. In the course of his lifetime, Tom's financial status ran from "poor" all the way up to "lower middle." During one period early in his life, he spent his nights baking little pies and his days standing on a corner selling them and dozing off now and then standing up. Things got slightly better after Tom came out of the Navy, but not all that much. At least he had a job. Like Mark, he ran into his share of tragedy, the toughest one being the accidental death of his fourteen-month-old son. Later, when he wrote to console a friend in *his* suffering, he mentioned in passing, "When tragedy strikes (as you know I have personally seen it strike many times)...."

All his life, Tom's top priority was trying to help others. So it was an established pattern when he gave his last nineteen years to working for and with the poor broken guys on Los Angeles' Skid Row, at a place known then as "Miserere [Mercy] House." He was kind to the men who drifted in there, boosted their egos, begged for them, fed them, fought for them, and even managed to help some of them get back on their feet and sometimes back home. In the meantime, he and his wife, Stacia, lived in a little shack of a house next to and owned by their parish church, where Stacia devoted her time to teaching special children.

Tom died as he had lived, calmly, peacefully, even cheer-fully. As one of his grandsons once wrote to him:

> While those around you bay and bicker, you shall always shine out with the good word on your tongue and the ever-present smile gracing your lips. Hat cockily tipped back and eyes agleaming. . . . If only more people would adopt your patience and understanding in the face of all hardship, your denial of even an inch of room for bitterness, then perhaps we would truly see peace on earth. Yours is a mighty and eternal influence. . . .

And, at the funeral, his pastor expressed Tom's secret: "His was such a gentle charm, such a beautiful, Christ-like appreciation of every person that he met."

Tom's Secret

Mark tried to be the standing-tall stoic, bravely enduring, without much reason for it, except maybe a kind of macho pride in his own outer courage. That isn't all bad, but it isn't enough either. To turn in on oneself, to use one's work as the only antidote for suffering, just won't hack it. So Mark finally took his own life.

Tom had the one thing necessary: faith. Or, as his pastor had put it, he was "Christ-like." Without faith, one can never handle human living over the long haul, especially maybe the tough parts, the so-called defeats. With faith—with God—one can handle and even make good use of *anything*.

That "mighty and eternal influence" Tom's grandson mentioned could have come only from faith.

Faith for Living

We need all kinds of faith in this life. You have to have faith that the Big Mac or the Pepsi isn't poisoned by some crazy. (It would be an added bonus if you could have complete faith that the stuff is good for you.) You have to have faith in your doctor and that he's giving you the right medicine. You have to have faith that the noise under your car's hood is telling you it will get you there, and not that it's about to blow up. You have to have faith, generally speaking at least, that people you deal with are honest and decent.

But these kinds of faith, while important for human balance, are not the basic, primary faith needed, the one we're discussing here: *faith in God*. Without that one, you can forget the others, because without that faith, your whole foundation will collapse. So will your mental balance. So will you.

Remember this: while life's unpleasant experiences (like suffering, *some* of which is inevitably going to hit you sooner or later, since this is not heaven), are always going to stay at least partial mysteries, still, with faith will come some hints of an explanation. The best clue, certainly, is to be found in the crucifixion, but even this is only, *for now*, a clue. The complete explanation will just have to wait. In a sense, faith is "waiting." But without it, we don't have a clue. Or a chance. As the apostle Paul put it: "We live by faith, not by sight" (2 Cor. 5:7).

But faith is necessary for a lot more than balanced living. It's necessary for humanity. Try to get rid of your faith and you cut off a part of yourself. To paraphrase one theologian: It is in recognizing a person's dependence on God that one sees aright. This relationship is not some kind of added truth (the frosting on the cake) glued onto a human being, who could exist just as well without it, but it's a *part* of being human. So a person who rejects this faith becomes mutilated in his very person, in his humanity. *A person without God is not fully human* [adapted from Jean Danielou].

All right, so that is a theologian talking. And someone's sure to say, even though it would be inaccurate, "He *has* to say that."

Okay, so let's take it from another viewpoint, a scientific one. A psychiatrist named Carl Jung (one of the two best-known pioneers in the field) was not at the time a "religious" man, only a hard-nosed scientist, but he put it this way:

> During the past thirty years people from all over the world have consulted me. Among all my patients...*there has not been one* whose problem in the last resort was not that of finding a religious outlook on life. *Every one of them* fell ill because he or she had lost that which the living religions of every age have given to their followers, and *none of them has been really healed* who did not regain his religious outlook [adapted].

Since all of Carl Jung's patients came to him, not because of a head cold, but because of some loose bolt rattling around in their brain, what he is saying is "You gotta be nuts not to have faith." Paul said the same thing more politely: "Everyone who is *spiritually mature* must think this way." Which should jerk you back to the first section of this book.

Maybe there's a connection here with the fact that loss of

faith has been found to be so closely related to drug abuse, that form of insanity so "popular" today. Or maybe the one who put it best, certainly most briefly, was the great stand-up comedian Henny Youngman: "I took up atheism, but had to give it up. No holidays." The unbeliever has nothing to celebrate, because, for him, there is no permanence, and even the fun things fade away, leaving nothing but memories. The believer, though, can relate everything, fun and games as well as duds and pains, to the eternal, the permanent. We can never be really and thoroughly happy without faith.

You just can't split yourself into parts and say, "I'm spiritually dead maybe, but psychologically I'm okay." No way. You're either an airhead spiritually and psychologically, or you're together in both departments. You're one united person, not a bunch of separable components. And so, the whole "you" is balanced or unbalanced. Faith is not, of course, just a sanity preservative. It's the human preservative, the nitty-gritty of your personhood.

Okay. . . so what is faith then? Well, basically it's the belief in God. It's a belief in what he's like—personal and, for some pretty mysterious reasons (at least on some days), in love with me. Faith is the belief that, no matter just how he did it, he is my Creator. And—as we'll get into in another chapter—he is my goal.

Maybe one of the most important things you have to keep in mind is that faith is not a "feeling." Remember what was said about maturity? It's acting on principle and conviction, using and controlling your emotions, but not letting them use and control you. That's really important, because if you believe only when you feel great about it, you're going to have a lot of vacuums in your "belief." Faith can, in fact, get pretty tough sometimes, and doubts can hit you hard. But that's normal and, in fact, necessary for faith. This cliché is true: "No doubts, no faith." All of us can relate to the cry of that concerned father in Mark 9:24: "I do believe; help me overcome my unbelief!"

It's the same way with prayer. If you only pray when you feel great about it, you've just cut off most of your prayer life.

No, faith is "I'm convinced," not "I feel." Of course, some days you may feel just great about that, but other days, although you will know and so have faith, you may still feel pretty rotten about everything.

The author of Hebrews laid it on the line: "To have faith is to be sure of the things we hope for, to be certain of the things we cannot see" (11:1, TEV). As Paul wrote: ". . . But what is seen is no hope at all. Who hopes for what he already has? But if we hope for what we do not yet have, we wait for it patiently" (Rom 8:24–25). So we're back to that connection between "faith" and "waiting" again!

There are a couple of other things it's important to remember about faith. First of all, it can't be forced on you. It has to be a *free choice of yours*, even when you seem convinced by all the "arguments from reason." Think about that a little bit, and you'll see that makes faith just like love (which, of course, faith is!) You can't force anybody to love you; nor can anybody force you to love them. In other words, we forever retain the right to make utter fools of ourselves! "The fool says in his heart, 'There is no God,'" (Ps. 14:1a).

Both the biggest brain and the biggest klutz have to "become children," in a sense, when it comes to faith. That's why a super brain like Mortimer Adler comes up with something like this:

> Interviewer: "If you were invited to deliver a sermon . . . to believers, what would be your basic message?"
> Adler: "I would say: Thank God for your belief and thank philosophy for showing you that it is not absurd."

One might add, "Thank your mind for letting you know how totally stupid it would be *not* to believe in God."

So . . . ?

If you haven't faith, or if you've lost it, it's time to search for it and hope the Lord will give it to you. You'll notice that this will suppose your effort and goodwill, for openers. If you do have faith, even though the doubts often hit on you, be grateful and guard it carefully. Once lost, really lost, it's awfully tough to get it back. In fact, most people who claim to lose faith are reasoning backwards, saying, "If I say I believe in God, then I have to believe in what he tells me to do. But I don't *want* (There are those emotions again!) to do some of the things he tells me to. So I'll just say he doesn't exist."

Now, as you can see, that's not even close to "reasonable." In fact, it's unbelievably stupid.

You want to be peaceful, calm, mature? Without faith, you can't possibly be any of those things. With faith, you most certainly can be all of them. Faith—far from being just a single act or even frequently repeating, "I believe"—is a way of life. You get the ammo for that way of life in your declarations of belief, in your other prayers, and in your practice of religion. Just about everywhere—if you're looking and listening.

But you don't just declare your faith. You *live* it.

7

"God Exists: No Doubt About It"

The Day It All Got Out of Sync

Even before anybody got a chance to say, "Have a good day," it was obvious that it wasn't going to be one. . . .

When Lola yawned her way out to the porch to pick up the morning paper, she was afraid (well, to be honest about it, she *hoped*) she was having a nightmare and would soon wake up. Sally the Squirrel had tipped over the milk-bottle and was lapping up the stuff like a cat, while Cleo the Cat was carefully stacking up nuts over by a tree. Somehow or other, a bear had wandered into the yard and was cowering in terror before a snarling rabbit. Terry the Turtle was out on the road chasing motorcycles. A mad bee was all tangled up in her efforts to spin a web, and a frustrated spider was stomping around trying to pull free of the honey it had tried to collect. Lola watched as Charlie the Chicken flew by, followed—in

flight—by a big catfish. A couple of robins were casually strolling down the road. Just when Lola thought she might wake up, Henry the Hummingbird, who had been her friend for months, savagely buzzed her head, until she fled into the house and slammed the door.

To make things even worse, the paper hadn't been delivered.

Lola pinched herself, unfortunately discovering that she was awake, as she watched water from the faucet squirt upward instead of flowing down, just before it quit entirely. She flipped on the electric stove, but nothing happened. And the fridge had seemingly been off for hours, with the freezer compartment dripping.

To Lola's relief, she managed to get a local TV station on her battery set. But her growing annoyance and puzzlement began to turn to fear when she heard that the TV station was operating on emergency battery-generator equipment, which, the announcer pointed out, would soon run down.

"*Something* is wrong," declared Jessica Mavrick, that always observant newsperson. "Nothing is acting right. Crops are rotting on the ground. The steers at the stockyards are pawing and snorting and charging the fences like mad bulls—so the food outlook for the near future may not be all that great at this point of time. And now," she added cheerfully, "here is our meteorologist, Dr. Kross, with the forecast. Are you going to give us some nice weather today, Kris?"

"Good morning, Jessica," Dr. Kross began cheerfully. "It's a mess out there," he laughed. "Man! In fact, we hear from the observatory that it isn't just earth that's all messed up—the whole universe seems to have gotten off sync. Professor Alfred Rhinestone reports that we are no longer spinning on our axis, and that the gravitational pull between earth and the sun seems to have quit, and we are drifting free, off into space. Wherever *that* is—ho, ho, ho! So bundle up, folks the forecast is for colder weather. *Lots* colder. . . .."

At that point, Dr. Kross's voice died, and so did Lola's TV. Just as the picture faded to a pinpoint, then nothingness, she heard the final cheery "Have a good day."

What Keeps It (*Made* It!) "Normal"?

We take it all for granted—that the water will flow in the right direction, the electricity will keep coming, the animals will act the way they're supposed to, and the universe will keep right on operating the way it always has. After all, we know that the earth in its annual trip around the sun at 65,000 mph has always made the trip in exactly 365.25 (plus just a tad more) days, never behind or ahead of schedule.

But we sure couldn't take it for granted if it just "happened," since (1) that would be a super stupid theory, and (2) even if it could have just "happened," it could just as easily have un-happened a long time ago. If someone has to put a spaceship into existence, orbit, and sync, a special "someone" sure had to have put this vast, complicated deal we call the universe into existence and kept it in sync, too. And all this, so far at least, despite mankind's tampering with the works.

From Nothing, You *Get* Nothing

Still, there are people who just don't want to face the facts, like the fact that the whole universe and everything in it is constantly screaming at us, "I *must* have had a Creator, or I wouldn't be here or operating smoothly—or at all! Come to think of it, I wouldn't be able to 'scream' either."

Yet there are people we call "atheists," who deny God's existence. More often, we have what are called "agnostics," who duck the whole all-important question with an "I don't know."

We probably don't have many true atheists at all, but we do have people who *say* they are, even some who have convinced themselves, over the long haul, that they really are. Now and then they slip a bit, like the Russian leader, then the world's Numero Uno Atheist, who once blurted out, "May God grant that we never have to use these horrible weapons." But why does anybody claim to be an atheist, or why are there people who may really have come to think they are?

The biggest "reason" is probably the one already mentioned, that if you do believe in God you have to "take the consequences"—like following his directions. And some people, like Adam and Eve, prefer their own "directions."

Then there are those who did believe in God until "something went wrong," and they told him (whom they claimed not to believe in!), "I'll show you—I won't believe you even exist." Not unlike the little guy who gets mad at his mother or father or both and says, "I'll show you—I'll run away from home."

Then, too, some people—mostly the medium-to-lesser brains billing themselves as "intellectuals"—demand a "reasonable proof" for God's existence as compulsive and unavoidable as two plus two equals four.

We have no choice but to believe that two and two really are four. We're forced into that "belief." But when it comes to belief in God we have to hack it by faith. God wants our *free* consent, our freely given faith—and our love. They go together.

We get the occasional sneer from the half-baked "intellectual" (often enough in that outlet of the frustrated writer, the Letters to the Editor column): "No thinking person believes in God anymore. . . . All intelligent people [like me?] disbelieve in God." But we can't help but notice that almost all great-minded people will tell you that they *do* believe in God. Nobody could ever confuse Mortimer Adler, for instance, with Mortimer Snerd. Yet Adler, this intellectual giant, made it clear: "God exists: no doubt about it" (*US Catholic* magazine, Oct. 1980). You have to pity the poor atheist. Like somebody said about the dead atheist lying in his coffin, "All dressed up and no place to go."

Actually, our belief in God seems inborn, built into us, so that a person has to work harder to lose faith than to keep it! Like Jesus said, "O Father. . .thank you for hiding the truth from those who think themselves so wise, and for revealing it to little children" (Matt. 11:25, LB).

In the preceding chapter, we saw in passing that it's really pretty unreal *not* to believe in God. With Paul, even though "full of doubts, we never despair." It's true, of course, that we can best learn to know our Creator from what he tells us in the Bible, and especially when, after a period of telling us about himself, he *shows* us himself, Jesus Christ. Still, we can't help seeing his hand—and thus his existence, and something of what he's like—all around us in his creation. As we look around, in fact, while we may not see or often understand what are supposed to be undeniable reasonable proofs of his existence, we have to say anyhow, "Hey, it would sure be really stupid *not* to believe."

Remember that Palm Sunday when Jesus was riding into Jerusalem on a burro, and the people were all giving him a big hand? The Pharisees told him to make his fans shut up, and all he answered was: "I tell you, if they keep quiet, the stones will cry out" (Luke 19:40). And so they do. But you won't hear them unless you listen.

The Stones *Do* Cry Out

"Stones"—pebbles and big rocks and mountains, blades of grass and leaves and trees and lakes, insects and animals and babies—they're all shouting at you: "My Creator put me here!"

A scientist knows that the chemical action in a single leaf is more complicated than what happens in the biggest nuclear power plant. And there are all those trillions of leaves. A tiny blade of grass has enough muscle to push its way up through the slightest crack in man-made concrete.

It's impossible—well, at least for anybody who allows "thinking" to cloud his or her mind—to look, really look at the mountains and lakes and trees (any trees, but how about those redwoods?) and streams (which you can also hear if you're listening) and not see the hand of our Creator at work.

When was the last time you really looked at the tiniest feather fallen from the smallest bird? Talk about perfection and symmetry! No human being could ever quite match it. Even if he tried, he'd do it in plastic. It could never be something that was once a part of life, that once grew.

If you've ever seen a spider web sparkling in the early morning dew (before you crashed into it, that is), you may have noticed that it's an unbelievable engineering job. The spider not only does it perfectly every time but takes great pains to repair it when the wind or some unnoticing slob has damaged it.

When you were little, you may have read E. B. White's *Charlotte's Web*. Charlotte, the spider, wrote messages in her web to eight-year-old Fern Arable. Fern's mother naturally got a little uptight when Fern told her about this, so Mother checked it out with Dr. Dorian.

"I don't understand," the doctor told her, "how a spider learned to spin a web in the first place. It's a miracle."

When Mrs. Arable protested that she didn't see what was so miraculous about a spider web, Dr. Dorian asked, "Ever try to spin one?"

Mrs. Arable answered, "No," but added that she *could* knit a sock. "But," the doctor persisted, "somebody taught you that, didn't they?" And, of course, she had to admit that her mother had taught her. "But," the doctor went on, "a young spider knows how to spin a web without any instructions from anybody. . . . Who taught the spider?"

Good question. Who *did* teach the spider?

And who taught the newly hatched snake to strike? Not his mother, because he never met her! Who teaches the butterflies who migrate to the same valley in Mexico each year by the thousands (and not one of them has ever been there before!) how to get there or why they're going there anyhow? Who taught beavers how to build dams or told them that's their thing?

Maybe you've been lucky enough to have watched a mother dog with her newborn pups. She's never had a class in natural childbirth, and yet she knows just what to do. So where did she learn that? Who taught her? And who told raccoons that its their job to spend so much time washing their food and rocks?

Dr. Lewis Thomas has been billed by *Time* magazine as "the best essayist on science anywhere in the world." In one of his essays, "Altruism: Self-Sacrifice for Others," he wonders, "Why should an animal, off on its own. . .choose to give up its life in aid of another being?'' He also points out that a bee can tell the time of day, calculate the geometry of the sun's position, argue with other bees about the best location for the next swarm. And he speaks of ''the genetic message'' as music, deploring our non- listening, our non-looking: ''Hard of hearing, we go to war. Stone deaf, we make thermonuclear missiles. Nonetheless, the music is there, waiting for more listeners.''

Oh, yes, you have to look and listen, or you miss the music God put there. But if you do look and listen, you'll know what Leonard Feeney, a neat poet, was getting at when he wrote: ''Snails obey the holy/Will of God slowly.''

We all know, though, that it's the human infant who most strongly (and sometimes with the most noise) forces us bigger human types to think of our Creator. Those neat little hands and feet, the heart pumping away, the lungs—and the eyes and ears already storing up information for future use. Even professional doctors and nurses, who should long ago have gotten used to this miracle, can't help being hit with it each time they see it. Like Dr. Thomas again:

> The true miracle . . . is . . . the union of egg and sperm and the emergence of a cell that can grow into a human brain. The mere existence of that cell should be one of the greatest astonishments of the earth. People ought to be walking around all day . . . calling to each other in endless wonderment, talking of nothing except that cell.

It All Just ''Happened''?

Oh, come on now!

There was a great song in an old musical, *Flower Drum Song*: ''A hundred million miracles are happening every day . . . .''

And so they are. If we're looking, we'll see them.

The stones *do* cry out, if we're listening! Like Hugh Noonan's great book title, *Listen, the Clams Are Talking!*

8

You *Can* Get There from Here

Window-Shopping

Tilly never seemed able to find much to do in the ghetto except get high. Especially after she dropped out of school. Sometimes she'd go across town and window-shop, but that only made things worse—looking at all those neat things she'd never have. Like the shiny cars in showrooms. Maybe someday she'd steal one, but that didn't seem too likely either. When Tilly had still been in school, she would go home and light up a joint—the stuff was as easy to get at school as Pepsi. The guys who had it weren't called "pushers" for nothing. In her later teens, though, she graduated to coke, then crack. Tilly didn't even know she was hooked (well, more like she didn't *admit* it) for a long time, and by then she didn't see how she could get unhooked. Besides, what else *was* there?

Jake wasn't surprised when this weekend began like most of the others. He came home from school and found two crisp hundred-dollar bills with his parents' note: "Off to Acapulco. Back Monday night. Have a good time." It wasn't always Acapulco, but it was usually some place away from home.

His parents were really good to him. They gave him all the money he needed or wanted, and he knew they were going to trade in his Ford on a BMW when he graduated. All they ever pushed him about was working hard to be a "success," like they were. But he was already sure of a job in his father's investment firm anyhow.

Jake drove around for a while, then went to a movie, but left part-way through when he realized he'd already seen it. He called his friend Gus, who said "Hey, let's go cruise Broadway and see what happens." Like everything else lately, though, that bored Jake, too. He thought about calling Lola, but she was acting funny, "different," these days. He was afraid she was getting interested in other guys. Besides, while she had a neat bod, sometimes he thought it only went as high as her neck. He drove around some more, hoping something interesting would happen, but nothing did. When he came back to the empty house about seven, he turned on the TV, then opened the cabinet and got out the Scotch. That didn't look so hot either, so he put it back. Then he went upstairs and reached back into his parents' dresser drawer for the coke they thought was safely stashed there. Carefully he laid out some of the happy dust on the table, rolled up one of the crisp hundred-dollar bills and sniffed. He had worried sometimes lately that he was hitting the stuff too often, but there wasn't anything else to do for excitement. He managed to rinse out his nostrils before the high hit him and he got sick and finally passed out. . . .

Oscar had never met Tilly, but their neighborhoods were the same. See one ghetto and you've seen them all—kids his age smoking joints, some of them sniffing or shooting coke, then crack. Lots of times his friends would offer him joints and dust, but he always managed to refuse. That meant he had to put up with a lot of guff like "Saint Oscar," and "How come you think you're so much better than us?"

Like Tilly, Oscar did some window-shopping, seeing all kinds of stuff he'd like to have in the store windows and car display rooms. For some reason or other, though, unlike Tilly, he didn't say, "I'll never get any of those things," but decided instead that maybe he would. As Oscar grew up, he began to understand that the shiny things he saw in the windows weren't all that important anyhow. So he worked hard at school, deciding he was going to get out of the ghetto and live, instead of lying around moaning and going to pot. And he made it. All during the near-despair he'd felt at times and the temptation to "get away from it all" with drugs or booze, one phrase had stuck in his mind: "Try God."

That he did. And it worked!

Drifting or Aiming

The drug-and-dope experts will tell you that "Drugs are the antidote for despair in the disadvantaged, and for apathy in the well-heeled." To translate that into English: When the only goals young people have are material, and (1) if they are wealthy and given everything they want, they may out of boredom ("I already *have* all that stuff"), try drugs as an "experience"; or (2) if they are in a total poverty situation, they may turn to drugs as an attempted "escape" from despair ("I can never *get* those things").

But rich kid or poor kid, there's nothing *forcing* either type of young person to be stupid enough to do dope. There are a couple of mysteries here, like why some of the biggest drug traffic is in the wealthier areas; and why one person "with everything" won't make it in life, while someone else from the most disadvantaged situation will make it.

There are lots of Oscars, for whom the answer is mainly in one word: *goals.* There's a lot more than drugs involved here. . . .

Goals and The Goal

West Point cadets are taught always to walk as if they were going somewhere, not just strolling around aimlessly. There is, of course, a time just to stroll, but it can't be a total lifestyle. That's the big difference between aiming and drifting: goals.

In every situation you live in, both now and in your future, without goals you're dead—at least from the shoulders up, with a good chance the rest will follow ahead of schedule. Like the title of an article about one of that prehistoric breed, a hippie who died in his twenties: HE LIVED. HE DIED. GROOVY. He went nowhere, accomplished nothing for himself or anyone else. A total zero.

You need some real, long-term real goals, at home, in your neighborhood, at school, in your dealings with everyone else. For example, if your only ambition concerning school is to finish it off (well, that's understandable, but not even a close second to the important school goals), that's about all you'll accomplish. Your school goal has to be "What can I get here that I can use for life?" And that doesn't mean just for money and other material goodies. It's for your own humanity, your personhood, your total future.

If a person's goals are only material and/or always only "fun and games," he or she will be forever immature, forever drifting, forever actually goal-less, and considerably less than human. Possessions and good times are important, of course, but they're not life. One collegian, asked what he intended to do during the spring break, answered, "I will be contributing to the consumption of a thousand beverages— The Goal." A coed (probably no coincidence) said, "We'll probably just relax and consume as many beverages as possible—hopefully a thousand between us.''

Now, helping to consume a thousand beverages may not be all bad, depending, of course, on how many "we" are, how long one takes to get the job done, and the nature of those "beverages." But that's not life. And the horror story of the spring-break plans of that first interviewee is in the words he added, "*The* Goal." That's a phony "goal," even for that hallowed rite known as "spring break."

The goal-less dream a lot. Or rather, daydream a lot, wasting a lot of their time in wishful thinking instead of doing and striving, instead of focusing on any worthwhile achievements. Lester dreams of becoming a pro football player, and Fanny dreams of being Madonna's successor. In the meantime, Les and Fan only lie around dreaming, not taking any positive steps to realize their ambitions, nor—more importantly—working out a backup plan in case Plan Number One (if they have one) should fall through.

There's nothing wrong with dreaming. In fact, to accomplish anything worthwhile you have to dream a bit. But then, along with the dream, you have to reach. As someone (Leo Suenens, probably among others) expressed it, "Happy are those who dream dreams...." But then he added the all-important "...and are *willing to pay the price* to make them come true." Without that pay-the-price bit, booze and drugs and cults and all kinds of weird, humanly degrading things crawl into the scene promising to be escapes from reality.

On a sometimes-less-serious, but still ridiculous, level, we're surrounded with ad-agency appeals to unreality, to an alleged heaven on earth, with no hint that the offer lacks permanence. Like so:

NEWMOBILE: IT'LL DRIVE YOU HAPPY

OLDPORT RESORT: WE WANT TO MAKE YOU HAPPY

GET AWAY TO IT ALL: FILTERHEAD ISLAND

MAKE YOUR VACATION HAPPY FOREVER AFTER.

HOLD FAST TO THE GOLDEN DAYS: TAN-PAN—BE A GODDESS OF
THE SUN

PRESENTING THE SENSUOUS RESORTS OF LOS LAGOS: SLIP
AWAY FROM CIVILIZATION AND INHIBITIONS AND REDIS-
COVER THE PLEASURES YOUR BODY WAS BORN FOR—LIKE A
CHILD OF NATURE

Well, more like a beached whale.

The goal: "Let's daydream a lot!"

Maybe the most important bit of reality for you to latch on
to right now is recognizing and admitting the difference
between means and ends, or goals. A car is not a goal, but a
means of getting places and, of course, for some fun of the
sane variety, too. You'll be happy to know that schooling is
not a goal either, only a means. Not even your church is a
goal. It's just a means to your only really important goal,
God—the goal for which all the other goals along the way are
to be used.

Think about it and you'll realize that everything is really a means, even those intermediate goals, the milestones of life (like graduations) that we achieve along the way. We believers use everything—our work, our study, our prayer, our pain and our fun—to get to our one and only final goal, God. Once you understand and buy that reality, you'll better understand the truth in St. Augustine's prayer: "You have made us for yourself, O Lord, and our hearts are restless until they rest in you."

If you try to lose yourself in all the fun and games, all the stupid dope and other "escapes" pushed at you, that restlessness will still be there bugging you. But when you aim yourself and all you do at God as your only and final goal, you'll have it made.

There's no other way.

You may be surprised to know—but it's true, I promise— that the vast majority of people, young people included, do exactly that. In the college paper quoted above, for example, another student said, "I am going on a service trip to San Luis. It's a good way to have a lot of fun, do something positive for someone, and not have to spend a lot of money. The people I'm going with seem really neat, so I am expecting a good break." Out of the 6,000 students at this particular university, only 75 hit the road for the Florida beaches. But many more students signed up for those community-service trips, using their break to work with the very poor, migrant workers, refugees, children, and the elderly.

Somewhere or Nowhere

Many adults always seem to be asking, "What's wrong with our young people?" This has, in fact, been a very popular adult question all the way down through every generation of history. For one thing, it keeps the adults from asking, "What's wrong with us?"

In a sense, there is something "wrong" with all of us. To put it less harshly, we're not perfect. We're limited human types *en route* to our goal, but not yet there. Some drift. Some go the wrong way, at least for a while. Jim Marshall, the great Vikings football player, picked up a fumble and ran ninety yards to the goal. The *wrong* goal!

Drive through a lovely California city that still has no by-pass and you'll see hitchhikers, mostly very young, all along the curbs. Okay, so what's wrong with that? Apart from being dangerous, the main thing wrong with it is that if you drive in the opposite direction a few days later, you'll see some of those same hitchers going the other way!

They're not going *to* anything, only trying to go *away*. No goals.

A really great writer, Walter Farrell, began one of his books this way:

> The road that stretches before the feet of a person is a challenge to the heart long before it tests the strength of the legs. Our destiny is to run to the edge of the world and beyond, off into the darkness: sure for all our blindness, secure for all our helplessness, strong for all our weakness, gaily in love for all the pressure on our hearts [from *My Way of Life*].

To go *to* somewhere and *to* Someone. Not *away*, to nowhere and nothing.

9

OUR FATHER...

"A Friend Loves at All Times" (Prov. 17:17)

Milton Miller had worked hard all his life. Now, in his late forties, he was one of the world's top architects, with branch offices all over the world. He was a caring man who treated his employees like his own family.

Lately, Milton found himself getting fed up now and then with business details, so he and his wife, Melba, would sometimes get in their car and just drive. They loved to look at the beauty of the Lord's creation in Arizona and the autumn colors in New England. They especially enjoyed the breathtaking Sierra Madres and the warm people of Mexico.

This particular winter, Milton and Melba were driving through the Mojave Desert on the way to Santa Barbara, where they had a home and office. They stopped at a motel in Blythe, had a leisurely dinner, and then drove out into the desert, which, they knew, can be beautiful at night.

On an all-but-deserted road just outside of town, they came upon a stalled pickup and camper, so they stopped and asked the young couple if they could be of any help. They learned that Dan and Nancy had been married only recently and had both almost immediately lost their jobs with the John Deere Company back in Iowa. And now they were heading west, looking for work. "At least," Dan laughed, "we haven't had many heating bills out here."

After the desert—a paradise!

Milton sensed from their conversation that Dan had been a natural manager, good at dealing with employees. So, after he had checked them out, he hired both Dan and Nancy for his California branch. The Millers liked the young couple, so they set them up in a small but lovely old home in Santa Barbara, near a brook and with a neat yard and some avocado and orange and pear trees. After their weeks in the desert, it was just about everything Dan and Nancy wanted—shade, cool breezes, water, and, of course, jobs.

In fact, as Dan and Nancy got to know the Millers better, they came to regard them more as parents than as employers. It was mutual, and Milton and Melba soon regarded the young couple as the children they'd never had.

Things were going smoothly in the business, so Milton and Melba decided to spend some time in Mazatlan. During their absence, Herb, one of the Santa Barbara bookkeepers, casually remarked to Don and Nancy, "You know, this is a good deal we've got here with M and M, but we could do a lot better."

"What do you mean?" Nancy asked.

"Well, let's face it—he's getting older, and he really doesn't give all that much of a hoot about running the business anymore. I have an idea how we all could make a lot more money. And it looks like Dan's going to be the head honcho around here anyhow. All we have to do is change a few numbers."

Herb's "idea" sounded a lot like embezzlement, so the couple told him off in no uncertain terms. The longer Milton stayed away, though, the more they toyed with the idea, and the more attractive and less crooked it seemed to siphon off some bread for themselves, invest the money, and return the firm's funds after they took their profit.

So they moved a pencil here, another one there, as they shifted funds around so they could "borrow" them. Dan and Nancy were surprised but not too unhappy, when Herb disappeared after a few weeks. They were definitely unhappy though, when the investments that Herb had recommended went down the tube. Then, before they could put the firm's money back, Milton came home to discover what they'd been up to.

Milton and Melba were more than disappointed—more like heartbroken. They knew, though, that it wouldn't be fair to their other employees just to overlook it. So they fired Dan and Nancy. Naturally the young couple packed up and left that little house they had come to love.

Before the two headed for Sacramento to look for work, though, they were dumbfounded to receive a note saying that Milton had arranged for jobs for them in his Sacramento branch, not in high positions, but good enough. Not only that, but Milton had again gotten housing for them, furnished!

Love Is Like That

You think maybe Milton's an easy mark, a complete fool? Well, maybe, maybe not. . . .

Think back to the very beginning of Genesis. Remember, this book was given directly to people who lived in the desert. Mostly they had only sand, sun, scorching heat, and dryness, not a lot of water or shade or streams or neat things like that. (They had lots of oil but didn't know it, and they wouldn't have cared anyhow.)

If you tell a desert-dweller, "Okay, to show my love and care for you I'm going to give you anything you want," he'll say, "So come up with some shade and trees and streams and cool air now and then." So notice:

> Now the Lord God had planted a garden in the east in Eden, and there He put the man he had formed. And the Lord God made all kinds of trees grow out of the ground—trees that were pleasing to the eye and good for food. . . . A river watering the garden flowed from Eden. . . . Then [later] the man and his wife heard the sound of the Lord God as he was walking in the garden in the cool of the day. . . (Gen. 2:8–10; 3:8).

You know that story. It's really the same story as that of Dan and Nancy. Adam and Eve blew it, believing the snake when he told them that if they did what they wanted and ignored what God wanted, they would be able to take over from him and be "like gods." They dallied with the idea and finally fell for it.

So what did God do? Well, he had no choice but to "fire" them from that perfect setup he had given them at first. But he didn't stop loving and taking care of them. Notice this tender touch, especially after what they'd done: "The LORD

God made garments of skin for Adam and his wife and clothed them" (Gen. 3:21).

The Best Father You'll Ever Have

You can't make yourself go all-out for *any* goal if you don't know anything about it. And then, knowing it somewhat, you have to really want it. Which means that, in some sense, you'll have to love it. So if God's your only final goal, you'd better get to know and love *him.*

You start with the realization that God is not some "it," not some magnificent, potent blob of goodness, but a personal Someone. And a person who loves *you.*

You may have heard this cliche: "The Old Testament is a book of fear, but the New Testament is a book of love." And if you have heard it, forget it—it's only a half-truth. Both are books of love. And since both are God's Word, written and published for us by his human ghostwriters, they're usually packaged together.

In the Old Testament, God is gradually trying to *tell* us what he's like. In the New Testament, he goes far beyond that and *shows* us what he's like—in the only way we can really understand—by becoming one of us, Jesus Christ. Read the Old Testament, and mainly one word will keep flashing across your mind: *Father.*

Okay, if somebody asks for a footnote here: God is our Creator: so, in human terms, we can call him our Father *and* Mother—and, in fact, a lot more. The trouble is that a word like "Creator" doesn't get through to our affections. We can snuggle up, though, to "Father" or "Mother." God is trying to tell us in the Old Testament that he has all the great characteristics of a perfect parent. And since he would get as annoyed as any writer with having to constantly repeat "Father or Mother/he or she/his or her," and so as not to offend one or the other gender, he wisely settled on one word—"Father"—figuring we'd have sense enough to know what he meant.

But if it turns you on, you can think "Mother" instead.

Those parents we are most familiar with, our own, usually run from great to not-so-great to zip. None of them is perfect. All humans have some faults. Sometimes they make mistakes. Now and then, in fact, the mistakes are whoppers. As one divorcee with a six-year-old daughter wrote: "How can I tell my daughter that God is a loving father, when she hasn't seen the clown who is her own father since she was a baby?" There are, of course, two sides to every question, and this is only one. Obviously, too, at some point of time, this woman hadn't regarded the guy as only a "clown." Even if the man really was and still is a klutz, though, she's missing something important here. Sometimes those kids whose father is either long gone, or they wish he were, will have a good idea of what the ideal father would be. A better idea sometimes than those kids who have on the premises a selfless father they've come to take for granted.

So let's think about the qualities a good parent ought to have, realizing that most parents do have most of them, maybe more obvious on some days than on others. And we'll stick, like the Lord himself did, with "Father."

A father *loves*. Okay, so that seems obvious. The thing you may not have thought of lately, though, is that a real father loves even *before* he's met his child. The main reason he cooperates with the Lord in bringing the child into existence is that already, though vaguely, he loves and wants this child, this person. In that sense, a human father shares in God's creativity, and in God's loving all his children even before our actual existence!

Once the child exists, a father *cares for* him or her. A father *provides* for his child, sometimes having to be physically away from the child quite a bit in order to manage it. But he *shares* what he has with his child, and when he can, he shares himself and his time. In so providing, fathers get the wherewithal to feed and clothe the child, so they have come to be known as "breadwinners." Mother, too, has always "won some bread," maybe more obviously so today.

A father will *guard and protect* his child, *defending* the child, should that be necessary.

A good father is *self-sacrificing*, not self-centered but *self-less*, putting his child's good ahead of his own.

A good father will *inspire—leading and encouraging* his child mostly by his example, by the way he himself lives. And so a father, often without words, *teaches*.

In teaching—and if you think about it you'll know this has to be—a father has to *lay down certain rules*. He doesn't do this just to throw his weight around and show he's the boss, but for the good, protection, and maturing of his child. To neglect this responsibility would make him much less of a real father.

But a father also *listens* to his child, and takes into consideration what he hears.

Human nature being what it is, a father will sometimes have to *forgive* his child (and, of course, that child may sometimes have to forgive his or her father!).

A father will sometimes *worry* about his child. Sometimes, too, when the child seems to misunderstand and to reject his love, a father will *cry*, although he'll probably make sure first that nobody's around to see it.

Loving "Anyhow"

Maybe the most important thing for any of us to hang on to, though, is that a father loves his child *anyhow*, no matter how stupid or ungrateful that child might sometimes be in action. A real father never quits as a father. Never. Being a perfect parent, he knows, does not require forever-perfect children.

And right there you have the main reason it's so ridiculous to dub the Old Testament "a book of fear." It's no big deal to "love" one's children only up to their first or even tenth mistake. God—the perfect father—stays on as such despite any number of mistakes on our part. That's why the so-called delinquent girl (for example) really gets turned on when she comes to realize that God is her Father *anyhow*, no matter what. She's probably never met a father like that!

Humanly speaking, Joseph, husband of Mary, was the "perfect" father. He dedicated everything, his whole life, to his family and their welfare. Selfless. And he never even got a headline.

Okay, so add up all those great qualities of the ideal human father, and you will start to understand what God is like. Above all, *he loves*, and so, like a good human father, he gives us a lot more than necessities to show that love. God is the only perfect Father, with at least one major quality standing out over all the others. He's not just our all-loving and never quitting Father but is also all-knowing. And so, unlike any earthly father, God makes no mistakes, even when we, his kids, imagine he did!

All through the Old Testament we see stumblers, even those God chose as his special human agents—like Abraham, Moses, David, and such. They all fell flat on their respective faces at one time or another. But he always stayed on as their Father. And God will never quit being *our* Father, no matter how stupid we might sometimes be, no matter how often we stumble or fall.

So . . . ?

So, if God is our perfect Father, loving us "anyhow," no matter what, the least we can do is try to act like his children by loving him, believing and trusting him. Maybe, above all, we have to keep in mind that God is not just ready to pick us up when we fall, to forgive us without limit, but is forever "standing by," eager to do just that. That's his message to us in the Old Testament, a message he made all the more clear in the New Testament. Read again Christ's parable of the prodigal son (Luke 15:11–32, and you'll understand better "all of the above."

So let's look around and see where we've been, where we are, and where we might be going. . . .

In Part One we took a look inside ourselves, with only a hint now and then that there's some relationship to God inside there.

Then, here in Part Two, we stopped just hinting around and took a more direct look at ourselves as related to God. The big items we recalled were that we not only come from God, our Creator, but that he creates us in such a way that we can find our fulfillment and perfect happiness with him—in fact, finally *only* with him. He is our goal, as well as our beginning.

But far from being "only" some seemingly remote and seemingly impersonal Creator, God is very close to us, helping us along the way. He is, in a word, our perfect Father.

Next we're going to take a look at some of the means God gives us to succeed. Naturally, among those means will have to be his directions. So that's what we're going to take a shot at in Part Three.

This Is How
You Get There

We've progressed from taking a look at ourselves through the consideration of ourselves as related to God. We saw that our relationship to him is that of children to a Father, not just any old father, but one who not only loves us but knows everything, us included. So he knows what's good for us and treats us accordingly. Above all, we saw that God is our Father "no matter what," that he stays on as our Father no matter how silly or stupid we may sometimes choose to act. He's always around, not just ready, willing and able, but eager to welcome us back into his Fatherly arms.

Now we want to take a look at the directions God gives us for fulfilling ourselves, for reaching the goal for which he created us, our perfect happiness and fulfillment in and with him. We call those directions God's commandments or his "moral law." So we'll take a look at those directions, sneaking a look, as we go, at some of the sideroads that look easier than the main freeway, but that don't lead to him. We'll try to relate all this to what you've already been reminded of in this book, the means God gives you for making the right choices and thus following his directions to your destination. All that involves your dignity as a human being and your growing maturity toward responsible adulthood.

10

The Directions

Follow the Narrow Slick Road

By the time she was thirteen, Sandy's parents had given up on her. Well, more like *she* had given up on them, especially since her mother's third marriage, to Snark, a hophead who seemed to get Sandy and her mother mixed up sometimes.

So Sandy ran away. Again. This time she landed in the reformatory, and they just left her there.

Then one night Sandy got this phone call, from a Mr. and Mrs. Mahway. They said they had met her at the reformatory's Open House, and they were offering her their home—and, they said, their love. Sandy couldn't remember them, but, strangely enough, her built-in suspicion of adults was gone, at least as far as the Mahways were concerned, and she liked them right away, sight unseen.

"So when will you pick me up?" Sandy asked, resisting the impulse to add, "Could you make it in the next five minutes?"

There was a pause at the other end of the line. "Well," Mr.
Mahway answered finally, "we can arrange your release all
right, but you'll have to get here on your own."

Sandy didn't understand just why, but what the heck....
"So *how* do I get there?" she asked.

"It's really simple," Mrs. Mahway assured her. "Just keep
your mind and heart on where you're heading. Okay?"

"Yeh," Sandy answered uncertainly. "I guess so. But it's
pretty vague. Could you give me some directions—like what
way do I come, and—?"

"When you come out the front door of the jail," Mr.
Mahway told her, "just turn left, north that is, up into the
mountains."

"The mountains? Wow, that's a lot of work. You sure you
can't just pick me up?" There was no answer on that one, so
she went on. "Couldn't I go south instead, downhill?"

"Not if you want to get *here*," the man told her. "Besides,
that south area is 'mined'—all kinds of traps, muggers, even
killers. But the big thing is that we live up here, not down
there. Besides, we'll be watching out for you along the way.
I'll give you our phone number, and you can always call if
you run into any problems."

"It sure sounds a lot easier to go south, downhill,
though," Sandy muttered.

"True," the Mahways agreed. "Maybe," Mrs. Mahway
went on, sadly, "you'd sooner not come? No one's forcing
you, you know—it's only that we really love you and want
you with us. And we've got so many great things to share
with you, probably more than you could ever imagine."

Sandy believed her, so she did as she was told. She got
terribly tired sometimes along the way, and she fell a few
times. She was often tempted to turn around and take the
easier way downhill. But then she remembered that there
wasn't any home for her in that direction, so she got up and
kept climbing. Sometimes she had to call the Mahways for
new directions—like when she was surprised to find a big

gully in the way, and they directed her to a cableway she hadn't noticed.

Somehow, she kept going. And when she finally made it and met her new parents, she wondered why she had ever been stupid enough to even consider going the other way.

You *Can* Get There From Here...

...if, of course, you go in the right direction!

There was this sign at an access road along a major highway: "This Road Does NOT Go Through." The motorist unbelieving and stubborn enough to take it anyhow would see on the way back—in huge letters on the other side of the sign—"WELCOME BACK, STUPID!"

All of which reminds us of something we know well enough but don't always practice: "If you have a goal, head for *it*, not somewhere else. Follow the right directions."

If you skim through the Book of Exodus again, you'll see that the parable I call "Follow the Narrow Slick Road,"

parallels that historical and symbolic biblical account of the Israelites' exodus from Egypt. Like so:

1. The Israelites become enslaved in Egypt.
2. The Lord signs Moses as his agent, the visible leader to bring them out of slavery into freedom and to the Promised Land. (This happened around 1290–1260 B.C.)
3. The Lord "persuades" Pharaoh to spring them loose. Then he protects them all along the route, even tolerating their habitual griping and stumbling.
4. At Sinai, the Lord forms a pact (a covenant) with the Israelites, sealing it by the directions he gives them, known today as the Ten Commandments. Notice that he gives these instructions to a people he has already freed from slavery, telling them how they can *stay* free. As the apostle Paul was to say later: "It was for freedom that Christ has set us free. Stand firm, then, and do not let yourselves be burdened again by a yoke of slavery" (Gal. 5:1).

5. Follow these directions, God tells them, and you'll make it to the Promised Land. Blow them, and you can't possibly make it—you'll be going the wrong way.
6. The Israelites do stumble along the way, but the Lord

watches out for them, picking them up when they fall, and patching up his covenant with them.
7. So they make it to the Promised Land.

The Way To *Our* Goal

That's all history, sure. But it's symbolic, too—the story of our release from the slavery of sin, and the directions the Lord gives us for staying free and on course.

Our *only* true goal is God and the eternal home he offers us. We have no other. He gives us directions on how to get there—we call them his "commandments." Sometimes, from the very word, we look on them as "orders." But they are really (1) conditions, (2) directions, (3) liberators, and (4) protectors.

If you head in some other direction, you'll get *somewhere* all right, but not to your goal. Nor will there be any "Welcome Back, Stupid!" sign, because you won't be coming back. You only go around once. So the dumb thing to do would be to go some other way. The only smart thing to do is follow God's directions!

The only one who knows perfectly the way to our goal is God, our creator. Luckily for us, he's also our loving Father—so we're sure his directions are both accurate and in our best interests.

God gave us (in the Book of Deuteronomy and later through his Son) some very general directions, in what we call now the two great commandments: *You shall love the Lord your God with your whole heart, with your whole soul, and with all your mind.... You shall love your neighbor as yourself.* But that's a bit too general for most people so he spelled things out more in the Ten Commandments.

It would be a huge mistake to consider the Lord's directions as only his orders or as rules that various people along the line have dreamed up, just to be having a set of laws to show their clout. No, all God's commandments, whether given to us directly or indirectly, are really:

1. *conditions* ("*If* you want to get there, this is the way");
2. *directions* ("It's *this* way only, no other");
3. *liberators* ("These will set you *free* to make the trip"); and
4. *protectors* ("They'll *keep you free and safe* all along the way").

We humans can get all mixed up sometimes, often enough because our world and some of our own peers sometimes make us feel that the only important goals are material, sensually pleasurable, and self- centered, and that only nerds and wimps and their spiritual relatives look anywhere else. But our Father knows the right way for us to travel, and only he really cares just for *us.* Unlike our world and our peers, he gains or loses nothing from our choice—only *we* will profit or lose by our decisions. The propaganda bombarding our minds and hearts and senses may tend to distract and confuse us sometimes, but if we really want the right directions, they're always around and available, as God continually and clearly points the way. It's not always the easiest way, and it's seemingly uphill much of the time, but it's the *only* way to get to *the* goal we're made for: God.

Free and Secure

Besides being directions, God's commandments are liberators, freeing us from the very real slavery of sin and all that garbage. For example, from what you've seen and heard and read, even discounting the bragging rights, you must know about the dehumanizing slavery of being hooked on tobacco or pot or booze, or any of those big "adult thrills" (a misuse of words as bad as talking about "adult movies"!). But the slavery to a habit of sin—and some of the above can fall into that class—can be real slavery, not some figure of speech. The word *hooked* covers it well. Most of us shout a lot about "freedom," but the only way to be truly free is to follow the Lord's commandments. Otherwise, we're just locked in.

Besides being directions and liberators, the commandments are also protectors—not just from a re-enslavement to sin, but from other traps and dangers, too. Like if we could be sure, really sure, that everybody would always respect the commandment "Thou shalt not kill" and all it implies, we could walk around in our parks and streets at night without being afraid of being mugged. And we wouldn't always have to keep everything locked up and our homes dead-bolted to keep from being ripped off.

And Still Today . . .

Some people seem to have the attitude that, while the Lord's commandments were generally okay for those people way back in Bible times, they're outmoded today, so we can

It's harder to climb than to slide, but once you're at the top . . . WOW!

take or leave them. Which is like saying, "I would have accepted the directions the Lord handed out in 1200 B.C., and even maybe in 30 A.D., but I will not follow those old directions today."

But look at it this way: The goal is the same today as it always was. So the way to get there—the directions—must be the same, too. Otherwise, we end up somewhere else, as the Lord keeps reminding us. For example, isn't he giving us some very graphic evidence these days that there are dangers, maybe even penalties, for using sex as a toy instead of for sharing in a commitment of love and creativity?

The Lord wants everybody to reach eternal life, and Jesus didn't come to save only a tiny bunch of citizens who lived two thousand years ago. God sent his Son to save all of us. So how could he possibly mean his directions to apply only to the relatively few people of that historical period and only for those circumstances? It wouldn't have made historical sense for God to tell Adam, "Be nice to your mother-in-law," nor to warn Noah to observe twentieth-century maritime law. And even after Jesus had knocked Paul off his horse on the Damascus Freeway, he didn't need to say anything to him about not speeding through school zones. Nor did he go into the abortion matter, because it's only some vocalists of our present "culture" who have decided that the best way to cut down the population is to cut up unborn kids, and that, while others "shalt not kill," it's a mother's "right" to do away with her child—just so she gets the job done before the child manages to get born.

"Thou shalt not kill unborn children" is, however, not a new law that we can choose to disregard. It's only the Lord's original direction, "Thou shalt not kill," applied to all of us, young or old, sighted or unsighted, athlete or disabled, sick or well, beautiful or ugly, born or unborn. And the real horror story here is that we should have to be reminded!

Is There a Choice?

Even knowing that God's directions point us toward the *only* way to achieve our goal—that they are the only genuine liberators and the only real protectors there are—even then, we still have this thing called free will. We are, in fact, often tempted to aim at some other goal, to take that easier down-hill route, rather than the tougher climb upward to *him*, especially when we seem to have a lot of company, even some "friends," heading down that way.

But that's the way it's supposed to be—our choices, yes, and things and people sometimes trying to lead us in the wrong direction. But the Lord tops off all his other helps with the most important—and encouraging—one of all, *"I will be with you."*

Keep that in mind and you'll make the right choices, always going in the right direction. After all, God tells you the path to take, and he keeps you free to follow it, watching over you all the way.

11

"Sin" Is a Dirty Word

Chain Reactions

There was this neat garden, with lots of gorgeous trees and luscious fruit and stuff. The young couple who lived there were really happy. Well fed, too. They had been given only one order: "Leave that one scrawny little tree over there alone." After a while, though, they told each other "What we do is our own business, nobody else's." That seemed to make sense at the time, especially since there didn't seem to be anybody else around. So they sampled some fruit from that scrawny tree.

But, as we know, there was a whole human race coming up, every one of whom was affected by the decision this couple claimed to be "just our own business."

The couple had one son, then another. One day the younger son turned up missing, and his mother, after quite a search, finally came upon his body out in a field. She and her husband were really shook to learn that the boy's murderer was his own brother, especially when he told them, "The way I act is my own business."

They had heard that somewhere before.

That expression is still with us, as it was with this guy named Chuck. When he was in his teens, Chuck quit going to church on Sundays, partly because neither of his parents ever went anymore. He didn't question their explanation: "That's our business—nobody else's."

When Chuck quit church, so did his girlfriend, Nancy. Soon Nancy's friend Jane also quit, mostly because she was afraid that Nancy, and probably some others, would start calling her Goody Two Shoes. Sometimes Jane found herself worrying about it, especially when she saw some kids she admired still going, and when she didn't seem to have any-place to turn with her troubles and problems. But she always put the concern aside with "Well, it's my own business."

Chuck managed to get a college scholarship by a clever bit of cheating on the qualifying exam. "But it doesn't matter," he told himself, "everybody does it. It's my business." Hank, who had been nosed out for the scholarship, wouldn't have been so sure of that.

Chuck was proud of himself for usually "Saying No to Drugs." He knew only slobs did drugs, and he didn't want anybody looking on him as a slob. On the other hand, Chuck didn't feel it was anybody else's business that drugs were about all he did say no to. Nancy got worried now and then about their "relationship," never quite able to shake the thought that if she married somebody except Chuck (which she had a hunch she would), she'd be giving her husband only used merchandise. But then she'd think of Chuck's assurance that their relationship was "nobody else's business."

Eventually, of course, Chuck dumped Nancy, never even writing when he went off to college, still doing whatever he wanted because it was nobody's business but his. He was somewhat shook when he later heard that Nancy and Jane had killed themselves in a garage. The note they left said they were sorry, but that this suicide pact was "only our own business."

Chuck managed to shake the thought of Nancy, though, telling himself it *was* none of his business, only hers. One night, after he'd had a lot to drink (he never did say no to *all* drugs), he decided to give the girl with him an extra thrill by driving up an exit ramp onto the wrong side of the freeway. He managed to kill six people, the girl and himself included.

But then it wasn't anybody's business but his.

The Big Lie

You can forget the phony put-off, "It's nobody's business but mine," and the silly snobbery of "I did it *my* way." Both ideas are based on a lie.

The truth is that there is no such thing in the real world as something that is *only* your own business. Every action of every person has some effect, however hidden, on all mankind. Just as every good action, even every good thought, somehow betters the whole human race, so every rotten act, every mean little bit of selfish, stupid thinking, somehow detracts from the dignity and the well-being of the whole human race. The terrorist shames us all. Every person involved in the killing of an unborn child debases and disgraces us as a people and corrupts our humanity. (And it's even declared legal by some of our "leaders"!) Every liar, every cheat, every rapist, every unrepentant sinner of any variety—they somehow drag us all down, just as one tiny piece of litter along the road detracts from the beauty of the whole scene.

In the Old West, all kinds of treaties were signed, especially between settlers and Indians. Whenever some jerk violated the treaty, there would always be some who would point out, "But that was only one person." But, in reality, that one person's act reflected on a whole people. When one white person mistreated an Indian, the latter looked on it, not as an act of *a* white man, but of *the* white man. When an Indian retaliated, lots of the whites mistook *an* Indian for *those* Indians.

Sin: One Giant Step Backwards

Every sin a person commits, no matter how personal or well hidden, can never be entirely one's own business. Every single sin of every single human being pulls our whole race down a notch. Not one of us is as well off as he or she would have been without that sin.

Okay, so what *is* sin? Basically, it's anything done deliberately that turns one away from God. So it involves breaking one of his commandments—refusing to follow his directions, rejecting his offer of freedom, casting aside his protection. Sin is certainly ingratitude and, just as certainly, stupidity.

There are lots of other synonyms for sin, and we'll get into one of the biggies in the next chapter: immaturity. Sin is also an attempted escape from reality. A sinner, in his or her sin, is looking for something never to be found there—permanent, perfect happiness. So a sinner is being unrealistic, which is a synonym for at least "temporary insanity."

But that's the negative viewpoint. And while it's important to know what sin is, to be able to recognize it beneath its camouflages and so to avoid it, it's still more important and a lot more helpful to know what its opposite is: the faith and character and pride to keep God's commandments—which we sometimes call the moral law.

If you think about it, you'll realize that we would probably know those commandments, that moral law, even if the Lord hadn't taken the trouble to write them out for us. Any sane person knows it's wrong to murder or steal or cheat and lie or to treat sex like some toy instead of the clear responsibility it is. The Lord knows us so well, though, that he realizes we sometimes have to have things spelled out for us, even obvious things. Anybody in his right mind knows that it's stupid, dangerous, and immoral to drive through a school zone at 90 mph. But because there are kooks out there, the law has to be written down and penalties threatened for the crackpots who break it.

Moral law has to do with (1) a balance within oneself; (2) justice and peace and cooperation between individuals, to which we must all contribute if we're to be morally right; and, finally (3) the bettering of our race and human life as a whole. "Good" morality could be compared with a musician's playing the number the conductor wants, instead of blowing the whole beauty and harmony of a piece with "I'll play whatever I want—it's nobody's business but mine."

It would be a mistake, of course, to point to specific suffering as a direct result of or punishment for some specific sin. But it does seem certain that the Lord sometimes reminds us that his law is for both our personal and combined good. perhaps that's why things like Herpes and AIDS come along. A whole machine can get out of sync because of one loose cog. And it won't do any good to say, "I'll let it go on that way and patch things up with a few drops of oil."

The commandments and the Scriptures seem clear enough on what is sinful. All through history, though, there have been sneaky types trying to persuade us that immorality is not just fun—it's all right. Like much of today's media trash—constantly bombarding us with little more than immorality glorified. Sometimes governments try to play God and decree what is morally right or wrong. This identification of "moral" with "legal" was, in fact, one of the big factors in the fall of Old Rome. Just because you are handed a condom today by some government agency doesn't make it morally just dandy to use it. Some "celebrities" (they love that term), who always manage to "leak" their latest shack-up to the media (who, in turn, are only too eager to pass this priceless bit of information on to us) are not our moral guides. Nor are the polls and surveys that like to pretend that since (a) everybody's doing it, (b) that makes it morally okay.

Okay, then, so who is to be the definer of morality? Well, God is, of course. And, with him, you are. God and your conscience work together.

Unfortunately, sometimes the expression, "I'm following my conscience" has come to mean more like "I'm doing what I wish were right," instead of "...what I know is right." Your conscience can't be just a feeling or a wish, which you can turn any direction you want at the time; nor will it do you any good if it's based on ignorance.

Your conscience is your mind, judging (not feeling or wishing) what is right or wrong in a particular case. So, obviously, it has to know, and then be honest. And, to know, it has to be educated in the right way—like from Scripture and other good reading, from your church, from trusted counselors—not just from some ignorant nerd who only wants company on his skid downhill.

Someone has called conscience "the steering wheel of one's personality." And so it is. You really louse yourself up as a balanced, sane person when you ignore or try to warp or keep in ignorance that conscience.

But you and your conscience should concentrate more on "What is right?" (or even "What is better?") than on "What is wrong?" If you live positively, like the valuable person, the image of God that you are, evil won't find any room in you and won't waste your life for you. If you live strong, with principled and positive thoughts and actions, you won't be foolish enough or even have time to "play with fire." You'll also know the places, the circumstances, and the people who are most likely to pull you downward. So, being smart, you'll know that only the fool walks the very edge of a cliff.

The psalmist points out:

> The law of the LORD is perfect; it gives new strength. The commands of the LORD are trustworthy, giving wisdom to those who lack it. The laws of the LORD are right and those who obey are happy. The commands of the LORD are just and give understanding to the mind (Ps. 19:7–8, TEV).

And *all* really smart people know that, too.

Try as you will, of course, there will be times of weakness, maybe even failures. But then you show what you're made of—the strength of your faith, your courage, your humanity itself. You know that the Lord is not just willing but eager to forgive you—without limit. There are those around you, too, who may be of help at those times. Seek them out. Catholics, for example, believe in the "sacrament of reconciliation," whereby they not only seek and find forgiveness (with the priest forgiving in Christ's name, and so they have the assurance of hearing it aloud), but they can also get the advice they need for improvement, the encouragement they need to go on. Whatever your denomination, there are clergy and caring laypeople to whom you can turn to find that same support. There are helps, lots of them, within your horizons, in your own faith and religion. Above all, never forget the apostle John's words:

> I am writing this . . . so that you will not sin; but if anyone does sin, we have someone who pleads with the Father on our behalf—Jesus Christ, the righteous one. And Christ himself is the means by which our sins are forgiven, and not our sins only, but also the sins of everyone (1 John 2:1–2, TEV).

Lean on the Lord, no matter which human advisor you may or may not use. Only the Pharisees (whose successors, unfortunately, are still with us) were such blind snobs

that they claimed never to need forgiveness. We all do—
sometimes.

So...?

So spend your life *living* the good, clean, mature life,
which is not necessarily that "good life" held out to us by the
materialists and pleasure seekers. It's a waste to spend your
time on negatives—whether following the negative path
lined with drugs, sexual fun-and-games, whatever, or stew-
ing so much about the negatives in your life, like your faults,
that you miss all the positives, especially Jesus Christ.

When you pour water into a glass, it drives out the air. But
if you (being a scientific type who knows there's air in that
glass) try to drive out all the air *before* pouring in the water,
you'll never get a drink. Only, maybe, a lot of broken glass.

You might do well to ponder the words of C. S. Lewis:

> People often think of Christian morality as a kind of bargain in
> which God says, "If you keep a lot of rules, I'll reward you,
> and if you don't I'll do the other thing." I do not think that is
> the best way of looking at it. I would much rather say that
> every time you make a choice you are turning the central part
> of you, the part of you that chooses, into something a little
> different from what it was before. And taking your life as a
> whole, with all your innumerable choices, all your life long
> you are slowly turning this central thing either into a Heaven
> creature or into a hellish creature: either into a creature that is
> in harmony with God, and with other creatures, and with
> itself, or else into one that is in a state of war and hatred with
> God, and with its fellow creatures, and with itself. To be the
> one kind of creature is Heaven: that is, it is joy, and peace, and
> knowledge, and power. To be the other means madness,
> horror, idiocy, rage, impotence, and eternal loneliness. Each
> of us at each moment is progressing to the one state or the
> other [The Joyful Christian, pp. 123f.].

12

"The World Is My Toy"

Ask Dr. Dan Blander

"The World Is My Toy"

Dear Dr. Dan:

I have this thing, you know, about busting things. I see a little kid's toy on the sidewalk, you know, and I step on it. The guys I run with—well, you know, when we're bored we go around smashing windows. Sometimes we slash a few tires, you know. One night one of the guys brought along a .22 and we had a big time, you know, shooting out windshields and headlights. Sometimes we shoplift, but mostly we just like to break things, you know. I'm scared we'll get caught sometime, but I can't seem to stop it. And I can't let my friends down, you know. So what do I do?

AFRAID AT FOURTEEN

Grow up, kid.

Suicide's a Bummer

Dear Dr. Dan:

We (my friends and me) have been hearing about the kids' suiciding around the country. Okay? And a few of us have been thinking about it, and it sometimes come through pretty good. Okay? We got nothing to live for, not really, and the little bit of fun we do have is always getting cut short with the other hassles, like school and stuff. We've all tried pot and cocaine and like those, but they give you only a couple of minutes of high flying. Okay? Besides we been hearing about this Shirley Mac-Laine, and we figure she might be right on the reincarnation stuff. Okay? If she was a prostitute, like she says, in one of her previous lives, and she came back a big star, we might be in line for something better, too. Okay?

STUMPED AT SIXTEEN

Grow up, kid.

"Safe" Sex?

Dear Dr. Dan:

My boyfriend and I been going all the way, and I'm getting scared. Like I read about these teen pregnancies and stuff, and I'd be scared of an abortion. We been using the stuff they give us at school lately but I'm still scared. Besides, my guy sometimes forgets. And all we have is each other. So what do we do?

DATING AND MATING AT EIGHTEEN

Grow up, kid.

Scorn the Porn

Dear Dr. Dan:

I'm getting to be an old guy. I'm 60. But in some ways, I
guess I'm still an adolescent. I've been going to porno
movies regularly for a long time now, and, while they
turn me on okay, later on I always feel rotten for some
reason or other. Maybe it's because I can't wait to
get back to the theater, or maybe it's just that I can't
really afford them. But I'd like to get unhooked. Any
suggestions?

                              STILL STEAMING AT SIXTY

Grow up, kid.

Temper, Temper

Dear Dr. Dan:

I try and try not to, but I still keep losing my temper—
maybe ten times a day. Especially with my wife and
kids. The only peace I feel is at the corner tavern. And
that may be the only time they get any peace either. I
wish I could get over this. Only I don't know how.

FRUSTRATED FORTY

Grow up, kid.

One-Way Christianity

Dear Dr. Dan:

There's this broad (well, she *is*) I really hate, right? We
work in the same office, right? Every time I try to be nice
to her, like asking her if she'd like a cup of coffee, I get
hit with something like "Yeh, okay, so bring it over."
Like I was her servant, right? I'm worried about it, Dr.
Dan, because I always been a good Christian girl, and I
keep thinking about this "turn the other cheek" stuff
and all that, right? So . . . ?

TWENTY-FIVE, IN A BIND

Grow up, kid.

[Dr. Blander will be happy to answer your questions
and advise you on your problems. Write to Dr. Dan
Blander, P.O. Box PHD, c/o this newspaper. Dr. Blander
holds a doctorate in oversimplification from the University of Repetition.]

"Grow Up, Kid"?

Okay, so the above little piece of fiction was partly for fun. But there's some truth in the fun, too. . . .

First off, this may come as a surprise to some of the advice columnists, but they're not the final judges of morality. All they can give are personal opinions and sometimes advice. Much of what the better columnists come up with is, in fact, good advice. Unfortunately, some of their opinions (not always presented as *only* opinions) are simply wrong, sometimes even immoral. Like one prominent columnist decreeing that it's ridiculous to appeal to moral standards instead of condoms and implying that abortion is okay to take care of "accidents."

Obviously, Dr. Dan is not one of the major leaguers even in this game. It doesn't do much good simply to say, "Grow up, kid." You're trying to do that anyhow, and it isn't always that simple, as you know.

But even a clock that's stopped is right twice a day, and ole Dr. Dan did stumble on to a pebble of truth. The old guy getting his jollies out of porn movies is just as immature as the fourteen-year-old vandal type. And both are more than a tad weird—which is another word for "immature."

Yes, Grow Up!

What we want to get into here is the connection between sin and immaturity. There is one, you know, because sin affects personhood, making you less a real person, more a machine. (By the way, people who say sin makes you an animal are no animal lovers! Animals do not sin.) Sin warps your mental balance, smears up your dignity, the works.

Just being young has nothing to do with sin. If it did, all those little babies would be in even worse trouble than the rest of us. But being less mature than your actual age—well, let's think about that. . . .

Maturity comes in varying stages, and you *are* "mature" if your level of development fits your years. A baby reaches a certain stage of maturity when housebroken. As time goes on, though, that child can't be considered mature if his or her only claim to fame is knowing what a bathroom's for. The youngster who likes to watch nothing but TV cartoons on Saturday mornings (even though that's about all that's on) isn't acting immaturely. But if that's all his dad and mom enjoy, they've probably dropped a few cards out of their deck. The teen girl who doesn't really get mad when somebody whistles at her attractiveness is right on schedule—if, of course, that's only a *part* of life for her and not all of it. But if her tight-jeaned mother brags that "all the boys whistle at me because I look fifteen," she's slipping off her skateboard. Not to mention ignoring her mirror. There's a lot of difference between being young at heart and young in the head. Or, as someone has put it, "Don't be so open-minded that your brains fall out."

The great Jackie Robinson, the first black man to play baseball in the major leagues, pointed out, "A man must show moral restraint to win honors in the world of sport. The athlete who fails at self-policing automatically and foolishly eliminates himself from championship company." That doesn't need any proof, especially today when you notice all those drug busts. The immature drop out—not just out of sports, but out of life. They haven't the maturity for that "moral restraint," that "self-policing."

Briefly and simply, at least one connection between maturity and sin could go like this: Every sin is an immature act; but, of course, not every immature act is a sin. Usually it's just stupidity.

At this point, it might be a good idea for you to check back to chapter 2, on maturity. You'll notice right away that sin is an immature act, real "kid stuff." Maturity means controlling our emotions instead of letting them control us. Uncontrolled anger, for example, is both childish and, to some degree, sinful. Uncontrolled emotions of the immature—like envy and self-pity, prolonging grudges, causing or giving in to wrong-directional peer pressure, pride that has you looking down your nose at others, attempted escapes from reality through drugs or sex or whatever—are *all* kid stuff. And all, to some degree, are also sinful, since they all chop us up as human beings, as children of God. There is what they call a vicious circle here: immaturity feeds sin, and sinning prevents maturing.

If you don't think sin is kid stuff, take a look at one of its first cousins, crime: "The highest involvement in crime occurs among young men from the ages of 15–18" (*TIME*, 2/23/87). Dr. William Glasser, unlike "Dr. Dan Blander," is the real thing, among the best. For some years this psychiatrist worked with large numbers of lady criminals. His one essential demand of them was: "You must take responsibility for your own actions." And this seemingly simple challenge got incredibly positive results. His demand for responsibility is really a demand for maturity. In a foreword to Dr. Glasser's book, *Reality Therapy*, O. Hobart Mowrer points out that, for Dr. Glasser, "...all therapy is in one direction, that is *toward greater maturity*, conscientiousness, responsibility." We can see a similar connection with maturity in this description: "An irresponsible person may or may not do what he says, depending upon how he feels, the effort he has to make and what is in it for him." Sound familiar?

But Dr. Glasser knows very well that maturity and the moral law are also inseparable: "The objective of reality therapy is to support and strengthen, never to weaken, the functioning of conscience."

At a later date, Dr. Glasser applied his obviously successful theories to the public schools. His "reality therapy" combined with this "approach to discipline" produced these kinds of results, among others, in the schools involved:

SUSPENSIONS decreased 50 to 80% in junior and senior high schools; *FIGHTING* decreased 10 to 90% in elementary and junior high schools; *VANDALISM* decreased 40 to 90% in all of the secondary schools.

Irresponsible acting is immature—and it's sinful. That's it.

But let's just touch on a few real cases here, keeping in mind that each individual has to apply general principles like this one to his or her own self. Personal sin depends on lots of things, like one's conscience and knowledge and alertness at the time and such.

The teen guy (or gal) who makes a big vocal deal about "not believing in God," and so giving up on the practice of his faith—so he'll be looked on as "big man on campus" or a "rebel" or whatever—is acting immaturely and so is at least dipping into the area of sin. This sort of thing is about as genuine a proof of maturity as smoking, drinking, sex abuse, or driving a car. (Okay, so knowing how to drive a car is, in itself, "good." But to think it proves maturity is ridiculous and childish. There are clearly lots of emotional infants out there on the freeway.)

People who disregard the effect of their actions on others are being childish, immature, and possibly sinful. A young guy on a TV show told the emcee, "If I want to dance in the street, I'm going to dance in the street." He gave no thought at all to what that might do to others—like what if his dancing in the street blocked an ambulance?

Kid stuff! Possibly sin stuff. Not completely unlike the potential suicide who said he was often tempted to ram his car into an oncoming car, and when asked, "Have you ever thought of the driver of that other car?" answered, "Never." That's kid stuff of the worst kind. Also a crime. And definitely sin, double sin in this case: suicide and attempted murder. Also crazy.

Gossip, too, is kid stuff. The gossiper would be really teed off if *he* were the target, but he doesn't mind blowing someone else's rep. And so, sin can be involved here, hurting others *and* ultimately one's own good name.

Driving a car is a good means for getting places and sometimes even for fun. But driving a car immaturely, so as to carelessly endanger oneself and/or others is sinful, sometimes criminal, and always kid stuff. The little guy pushing his wagon carelessly may be only "acting his age." But the teen driving a car dangerously and carelessly is acting immaturely, irresponsibly, even sinfully. Not to mention insanely.

Mature people know very well that it's wrong to taunt others about their apparent drawbacks, limits, or defects (which really amounts to saying, "They're not exactly like *me*"). It's both rotten manners and bad morals. But this is a favorite sport of the immature. Sometimes they find this out, the hard way. There was this story about thirteen-year-old Nathan Faris of Dekalb, Missouri (reported in *Omaha World Herald*, March 1987). The boy was only a bit overweight. He was also smart, but not any genius. Yet, the *nicest* things he was called—and constantly—by some of his classmates were names like Chubby and Dictionary and Fang. The boy knew he was in for it every time he got on the bus or walked into a classroom. Brandon Crockett (twelve) reported: "We were on the bus Monday, Ernie and Earl and me, and we were calling him names. We should have stopped. I should have stopped them. I'm just sorry." Later that same day, Nathan pulled out his father's .45 and got off five rounds, killing a thirteen-year-old classmate and then himself.

Selfishness and self-centeredness may well be the hallmarks of the immature, who want to be the sun around which the world revolves. They see only others' faults, blame others instead of themselves, indulge in self-pity to the point of hating anyone who doesn't drop everything to rush to their aid. When you think of a teen girl threatening suicide because her boyfriend has discovered that there are others out there, you contrast with—to name just one of thousands—a

Susan Stevens, successful and compassionate lawyer, yet in a wheelchair all her life.

There isn't space right here to get into the immaturity involved in the abuse of sex, so let's settle for oversimplicity again. To treat sex as a toy, instead of as the lovely responsibility it is, will always be kid stuff, no matter what the age of the person involved. Certainly some of the most immature expressions among us have to be: "I don't see anything wrong in going all the way" and "It's okay if you're in love." Both of these expressions reveal not just immaturity, but an unbelievable degree of ignorance. And to call sexual intercourse "making love" tops even those other bloopers for immature madness. Any prostitute will laugh that one to scorn.

All those examples of immaturity are at least in the neighborhood of sin. They all involve a degrading of humanity, maybe even a destruction of personhood. It can be summed up positively like this: Only the mature know that love and sacrifice are inseparable, and that saying "I love you" is a lie if it really means "I love me—and what you can do for me." Not unlike the guy who says, "I love grapefruit," then proceeds to tear the thing apart, split it into pieces, chew it up, and swallow it. The grapefruit wouldn't exactly consider that love.

So . . . ?

So, take your time. Proceed on schedule. But *do* grow up!

13

Pressures: Good and Bad

Headline: FOUR TEENS ATTEMPT SUICIDE
IN APPARENT PACT

And the "attempt" succeeded. So Lisa, Cheryl, Tim, and John stand before the Lord God.

God: Aren't you four here quite a bit ahead of schedule?

Tom: Could be. But things got too rough down there.

God: Too rough? How?

John: We four didn't mind each other. But nobody else seemed to like us.

God: Hmmm. Not all that surprising. But that's *it*?

Cheryl: My marriage went on the rocks.

Lisa: Ralph, my boyfriend, dumped me for Jane.

God: Jane's probably a real dog, huh?

Tom: Not really. Jane's okay. But Ralph should have been faithful to Lisa.

God: Well, it's a bit early for monopolies. But how come you're here so early? Everybody down there puts up with more than that.

Tom: I caught hell from my parents every time the report cards came out. They wanted a genius, I guess. My old man kept telling me I'd never make the kind of bread he makes unless I shaped up.

God: I can see that would hurt a bit. But suicide? How about you, John? Your parents force you into this, too?

John: Not really. I started doing dope, then tried to give it up. But I couldn't. The lows were too much, and not even the highs were any good.

God: So how come you did drugs in the first place?

John: All the kids did it. I didn't want to be a nerd.

God: And you, Cheryl? I suppose somebody pushed you into doing drugs, too?

Cheryl: Not really. But when the big bang hit my marriage, drugs were all I could think of.

God: This marriage of yours—pretty young, weren't you?

Cheryl: Yeh, but Kathy got married, so when I got the chance so did I. I didn't want her lording it over me.

God: What about you, Lisa? How come you got tied down to one guy in the first place?

Lisa: You kidding? All the kids pair off. I didn't want to be the only oddball.

God: So . . . What we have here is Tom pressured by his
          parents; Cheryl pressured by another girl's mar-
          riage; John pressured to be "one of the guys";
          Lisa pressured by the other kids into being
          Ralph's girlfriend. Period. So all of you did this
          thing because of somebody who pushed you into
          it? [When all nod, the Lord goes on:] Let's see
          now—maybe you can remember how one of the
          big universities down there was hit with penal-
          ties because of their violations of the athletic
          code?

Tom: Yeh, I remember. A Texas college. The football
          guys were given cars and all sorts of neat things
          by the alumni.

John: And some of the big shots at the university and
          even the governor knew all about it.

God: And do you remember what the NCAA did to
          those young guys who *accepted* all that loot,
          even though they knew it was wrong?

John: Why, nothing. In fact, they got it made—they
        were all picked up by other schools.

God: And do you think that's fair?

Tom: Well, not really. They didn't *have* to accept the
        stuff.

God: And even with all the pressures, *you* didn't have
        to kill yourselves either. None of those pressur-
        ing you *killed* you; none of them *made* you kill
        yourselves. In fact, not a single one of them or
        anyone else even suggested you kill yourselves.
        It was the decision of each one of you, nobody
        else. Right?

John: So we're sunk, huh?

God: Well, at the very least there is the possibility of a
        temporary-insanity plea. And at worst. . . .

Choices

Nobody can judge the degree of blame in a suicide, because a human being has to be at least temporarily nuts to do
it. In fact, the teens in the above news item (and it's real, as
you probably know) loaded up on booze and cocaine just
before blast-off. They were obviously mentally disturbed
kids.

And nobody forced the college football prospects to *accept*
any of the crooked goodies offered them. No matter what the
pressures (and admittedly, for a poor kid, a flashy car is no
small temptation), they still had their own free will, to
choose or not to choose.

There's always pressure to choose wrong, and we're always free to do so. But we're also always free to choose *right*.

Every now and then, especially when the other news is not
very exciting, the press makes a big thing out of teen sui-
cides. And even though only a very few teens are ever this

crazy, the word *epidemic* crops up fairly often. Fortunately, the vast majority of teens know very well that pressure of one kind or another, real or imagined, is only a fact of life to be dealt with *all through life*.

You don't win the high or low hurdles by running around them. So you deal with pressures by (1) facing them honestly; (2) using your faith and trust in the Lord; and (3) taking pride in being your own sane, reasonable person. That free will of yours is yours alone, and nobody, not even God, can take it over. It's one of the major components in your own unique and valuable individuality. We can boil it all down to this one "commandment": It's our job to follow our faith and social standards in a world that often seems to prefer paganism and materialism, and so seems to be pressuring us into conformity (actually more like slavery).

Pressures: Legal and Illegal

There are good pressures and bad ones, just and unjust. Let's face it—most parents do pressure their children, one way or another. And the "pressure" from a caring, sensitive parent to have you do well (your best, in fact) is necessary and right and one of their responsibilities as parents. We all need an occasional shove. It becomes wrong if a parent pressures you to do better than your personal best, or tries to cram you into a category—a state of life, a vocation, a profession—that you know is not for you.

Teachers, too, will sometimes put pressure on you, especially to use what you have and do better than you're currently doing with it. But that's their job! And in doing it they do show they care. Schooling itself has its pressures: exams, assignments due, good conduct, whatever.

But notice, genuine pressure, both good and bad, comes from within you, even if sometimes inspired from outside. And so there's nothing here you can't handle. Actually, there will no inner pressure unless you've left the door open.

The media will sometimes pressure you, often trying to get you to imagine that it's "in" to be like the teen caricatures they show in "teen movies." Of course, what they are using is the pressure you're most concerned with right now—the variety known as "peer pressure." Since we're trying, in this section, to deal with some practical details of the moral law, let's get at the possible rights and wrongs of peer pressure. Starting with the wrongs....

Teen pressure hits you through your peers' attitudes and actions, their example or sometimes only their words. The threat of ridicule may, in fact, never be voiced aloud—although there may be the unspoken understanding that unless you conform to a certain image, you're not going to be thought worth bothering with, nor "welcomed into the club."

Maybe, for openers, one of the most important elements in your dealing with peer pressure is a certain depth perception, the realization that a huge percentage of the bragging you hear from some ("Man, did we make out last night." Or, "I drank a whole bottle of wine.") is straight fiction. Even if it were true, much of it is something a human being should be ashamed of, rather than brag about. And *that* insight of yours will be one proof that you're maturing on schedule.

All right, so we're talking here about sin. Where does it come into peer pressure? Or does it?

Well, first of all there's the deliberate pressurer, the guy or gal who will ridicule you by word or example if you refuse to go along with their wrongdoing. If their pressuring you to do wrong *is* deliberate, we're talking about a variety of sin known, among others, as "scandal." And Jesus had something not all that gentle to say about scandal, about people who willfully lure others into misbehavior:

"... it would be better for him [who causes one of these little ones who believe in me to sin] to have a large millstone hung

around his neck and to be drowned in the depths of the sea.
Woe to the world because of the things that cause people to
sin! Such things [scandal] must come, but woe to the man
through whom they come!'' (Matt. 18:6–7).

So the guy or girl who leads someone to sin, whether by
example or word, is in big, big trouble with the Lord—and
had better be an impossibly great swimmer!

But what about the victim, the character who is pressured?
What if some poor guy, in order to avoid possible ridicule or
non-acceptance, does do something he knows is wrong? If
you think about it, you'll realize that, while the pressure
might reduce the blame, it can't take it away altogether.
Nobody has taken over this victim's free will. Nobody can.

Deflating the Pressure

You have a lot of ammo to fight peer pressure that pushes
you in the wrong direction. First of all there's yourself, your
own dignity and self-esteem. Some good scientific studies
have shown that ''a disproportionate number of peer-ori-
ented youth hold themselves in low esteem and take a negative view of life. . . .'' (Five Cries of Youth, Strommen, p.
117). English translation: ''If you downgrade yourself and
your human dignity, you'll be a sucker for the loudmouth.''
Time, in an article titled ''When the Date Turns Into Rape''
(3/23/87), pointed out this same fact: ''Compared with other
women, the victims [of ''date rape''] generally suffer from
lower self-esteem and are not very good at asserting themselves. One woman, raped by her date at a fraternity party,
said she decided not to scream for help because she did not
want to embarrass the rapist.''

Your parents can be a big help—if you choose to use them!
When all else fails, you can tell the pressurer, ''I'd like to do
that, but my tough parents won't let me.''That's but one of

the good things parents are for—to be fall guys when necessary.

There's another great big help you may be overlooking— your own peers! The great majority of them are going the right direction and setting the right kind of example for you, although sometimes they may be too quiet about it. Even the loudmouth who is forever deriding the good guys really admires them, but he's afraid to admit it. He secretly wishes he were more like them, but because he lacks self-esteem, he tries to get a crowd to join his negativism instead of making an effort to change for the better.

Yes, you can get all kinds of support from your peers, those you know and trust and who are maturing the way you yourself want to. Be open to their friendship, their concern, their generosity, their example, their part as role models you want to imitate. Sometimes, in fact, your peers can be your best "instructors." In the many arguments over sex education in the schools, you often hear adults saying, "Better to learn it there than in the gutter," where by "gutter" they usually mean your peers. It's true, of course, that the loudest "experts" on this subject among your peers are completely untrustworthy. But it could be that some of your peers can do a better job of giving you correct information and right attitudes than some of those official teachers!

The teens in one city decided that collecting food baskets for the poor at Thanksgiving and Christmas was a good idea but just not enough. So they began working directly in poor homes on weekends, scrubbing, cooking, painting, the works—none of which, of course, they would do in their own homes. When asked to describe the project, the boy who had started it all got up and told about seventy-five of his peers, "This is the greatest Christian project we've tried. But if you aren't going to do it for the sake of Christ and because you see Christ in these people, forget it. You can't hack it long just to be thought of as a nice guy."

So...?

All right, so there's another side to the coin. We've been going on here about the peers who pressure you one way or the other, especially those who set you a good example, one you'd really like to follow. The reverse of that coin is your responsibility to be that same sort of example, a role model for others.

Let's review again.... First we took a look at ourselves, what we're like. Next we looked at God, what he's like and how we relate to him. In the section just completed, we examined his commandments, his directions, seeing how we can follow them, especially in some special circumstances. What it comes down to is our making use of the gifts God has given us—our faith, our unique personhood and dignity, our growing maturity. Now we will get at our relationship to others, which, of course, has much to do with our relationship to the Lord. In other words, what we're really about to do next is try to get at something we've been discussing indirectly all along: What does it mean to be a *Christian*?

PART FOUR

...And Bring a Friend

It might be a good idea to check out where we are just now, so you can get an idea of the whole picture and not imagine this is only a collection of scattered, if sometimes pious, thoughts. Our first consideration in this book was ourselves (as usual!). It didn't take long, though, to realize that we couldn't understand that whole "self" without being aware of our relationship to God, our Creator and our Father—and the goal of our lives. Understanding his fatherly love for us, we then looked at the directions he gives us to live our lives to the full, as he intended.

Now, we'll fill in the picture with its practical segment: living it! Obviously, since we claim to be Christians, we either live it as such, or we're lying hypocrites.

And "living it" means that somehow we must reflect

Christ in our lives, seeing him, too, in others—so that we act the way he would toward them. We are, Paul wrote, "Christ's ambassadors, as though God were making his appeal through us" (1 Cor. 5:20). And the Lord, with his usual clarity and bluntness, told us ". . . whatever you did for one of the least of these brothers of mine, you did for me" (Matt. 25:40).

So here we'll try to think out our dealings, as Christians, with others. The first such "dealing" is naturally that of friendship. And that, of course, will involve to some extent friendship's closest relative, love. If our friendships and loves are really genuine (and so Christian-based), this will affect our choices and decisions, causing them to be made from a Christian viewpoint and attitude.

Finally, we'll try to see what it really means to "be Christ" for others—instead of only piously proclaiming that we are! So let's get on with it!

". . . for his sake I have thrown everything away; I consider it all as mere garbage, so that I may gain Christ" (Phil. 3:8, TEV).

14

Friends and Enemies

"Love Your Enemy—It'll Drive Him Crazy!"

Herb wasn't the most popular kid in the school, but he had a fair number of friends, both boys and girls. He wasn't a starter, but he was on the basketball team, so those guys were his friends. So were some of the other kids he met around school and in his neighborhood. Herb could afford to be a bit choosy, accepting the company of those he enjoyed and ignoring those he didn't especially like or know. Now and then, in fact, he had to be blunt about it and make it clear to some wimp that he didn't want the guy around. Like those who were boring, or sort of strange compared with the campus hot-shots, or maybe the ugly ones. He liked better the flare of the guys on the team and some of the other biggies on campus, and he liked to be seen with them. The biggest wimp he had to deal with was Fred, the problem being that Fred seemed to like his company. The guy would walk along the halls talking to Herb until the class bell called him off.

Herb thought he'd finally gotten rid of Fred when he let him know how he felt, mostly by turning his back on the guy in mid-sentence to go talk with somebody else. It seemed to work, but not perfectly. Fred didn't tag along talking to him anymore. But every time they passed, Fred would greet him with the same old embarrassing enthusiasm, sometimes yelling "Hi, Herb!" from all the way down the hall.

After his junior-year basketball season, Herb had a lot of spare time on his hands. With the help of a few friends, and a generous allowance from his no-questions-asked parents, he got into the booze sort of heavy. Then heavier. At first it was beer, but then he graduated to vodka and bourbon and whatever happened to be available. By his senior year, there was no more basketball for Herb. He was a closet alcoholic and in rotten shape.

His buddies seemed to get along okay, at least for the time, but Herb was so hooked on booze that all he thought about was the next drink. Since his parents were gone most of the time anyhow, it wasn't that tough to keep booze around so he could drink all he wanted over the weekend and even on school nights.

One weekend, when his parents did happen to be home, Herb decided it would be safer if he did his boozing out of the house, so he splurged and rented a suite of rooms in a hotel downtown. That Saturday morning he was terrified to hear a familiar "Hi, Herb!" through his hangover as he was walking into the hotel lobby with a fresh bottle. Just his luck—it was Fred. He couldn't seem to shake the guy this time; besides, he was anxious to take the cure with a drink. Because he figured maybe Fred would be less boring bombed, Herb invited him up for a drink. Fred refused but said he'd like to see Herb's hotel rooms, and there really was no way to turn the guy off. Anyhow, Herb figured that once he started drinking, Fred would probably flake off.

By eleven that morning, Herb was so crocked that he passed out on the bed. When he woke up to the glare of an

"If your enemy is hungry, feed him; if he is thirsty, give him something
to drink: by doing this you will heap burning coals upon his head."

overhead light, he realized he'd been out for a few hours
because his watch said 2:05. So he managed to get unsteadily
to his feet and headed for the kitchenette, the only thought in
his mind being another drink. En route, he noticed how dark
it was in the other room, even though the shades were up, so
he knew that it wasn't two P.M. Saturday, but two A.M.
Sunday!

As Herb weaved his way through the living room to the

kitchenette, Fred's familiar voice came out of the darkness from the direction of the sofa, "I thought you might need me, Herb, so I stuck around."

Herb never had another drink in his life. And he had learned a lot more about what a real friend is. Like somebody who keeps trying to be your friend, no matter how you treat him, and who cares enough to stick around for maybe fifteen hours in case you might need help.

You've probably seen that bumper sticker: "Love Your Enemy—It'll Drive Him Crazy." Maybe even "crazy" enough to recognize a friend—and Christ—when he sees them.

The Man Within

Sure, it's kicks to be with the fun guys and girls. It's natural, too, to want to be seen with the stars instead of only the stagehands. But you can't tell what's inside by seeing only the stars' glittering wrappings or the stagehands' brown-bag packaging. But it's that "within" stuff that counts. And it lasts long after the wrappings are discarded.

The very immature judge people only by appearances. Those who are maturing on schedule don't really care what someone looks like; all they care about is what a person *is*, and that's inside. Which explains why race or any other kind of prejudice is a form of gross immaturity, while the truly mature are basically color-blind and have a built-in kind of X-ray vision.

There are lots of Freds out there. You just have to be sharp enough to look beneath the surface to identify them.

Unmasking the Phonies

"A faithful friend is beyond price; his worth is more than money can buy" (Sirach 6:15). Ever heard that one? It means, of course, that friends are a very important item in everyone's life. *Real* friends, that is, not the phonies who are only playing a role.

There's a prayer that ends with "No one is a stranger, unless I choose to make him so." It's true—everyone has at least the potential of being your friend. This means that there can be friendships, in differing degrees, between those of the same or different ages, boys and girls or men and women, and between people of all races and nationalities and faith practices.

So what *is* this thing known as "friendship"? Well, whenever the big thinkers are stumped for a definition, they come up with "We can't define it, but we can try to describe it." So let's borrow that idea. . . .

Most people would probably say that friendship means "Well, I like that person, and he [or she] likes me." True enough. But *not* enough. Friendship involves a lot more than that. Check out some of the qualities of any genuine friendship and you'll learn a lot more about what it is. It would be pretty simpleminded (stupid, really) to call it a friendship when the "friends" drag each other down, harming one another, like morally for instance. With friends like that, how would we recognize our "enemies"?

You can't honestly call someone your friend if he or she encourages you to shoplift or do drugs or other such no-nos. And maybe the worst blooper in this category is the guy who tells a girl that if she really likes him, she'll go all the way with him. And if she doesn't so "prove" her friendship, he'll dump her. So guess who really should get dumped!

There has to be some solid base of agreement between friends on root attitudes and principles, on the big important things. Friends agree on the biggies and are willing to agree to discuss (not fight about!) the lesser issues. For instance, not that it's all that much "lesser," but two people could still be friends and disagree on political candidates!

Maybe the most important requirement for a real friend-

ship is the sometime willingness to endure some incon-
venience, to sacrifice one's own wishes. In fact, if it's a
genuine friendship, at least a real *Christian* friendship, this
willingness will be strong enough to keep the sacrificer from
counting what, if anything, is the return on these "investments." To be a real friend, you aren't in the thing for
yourself, but are thinking first and foremost about what good
you can offer the other. The person who says, "I like you,"
but who isn't about to make any sacrifices, is only a pathetic
liar.

As you consider those qualities of a good friendship,
you'll probably be thinking that they will also have to be
necessary in love, especially in the kind of love that leads to
marriage. That show-business genius, the late Billy Rose,
knew a lot about marriage, especially about why they break
up, since he'd helped to break up five of his own! "The
reason marriages break up," he wrote, "is that the man and
woman are simply not *friends.*" Married people either
become better and better friends as time goes by or their
marriage will self-destruct, sooner or later.

There's a lot of faith involved in real friendships—a basic
faith in the Lord, of course, but also faith in each other. And
that means trust. A side effect of trust is a loyalty strong
enough, for instance, to cause someone who has stumbled
into a gossip session, to say, "Hey, that's my friend you're
talking about!" So along comes courage, too.

Friendship, like love, is voluntary. Nobody can force you
to love or to be his or her friend. Nor can you force anybody to
be your friend. You can persuade someone maybe, but not
force. If you could, that wouldn't turn out to be either love or
friendship. As time goes by, you'll discover that some of the
people you meet, who at first either turn you off or just leave
you cold, may turn out later to be very good friends. Some
laid-back people grow on us and last better than the life-of-
the-party types who act like they want to be everybody's best
friend—on the surface.

No Strings Attached

Friendship, along with that spirit of self-sacrifice, demands generosity. You can't just bounce *yourself* off your friends, implying, "What can you do for *me*?" Friends are not to be used to glorify oneself. Maybe it's part of what Christ meant by telling us he didn't come to be served but to serve, adding that *we* will only be "the greatest" if, like him, we become servants. The generosity of a real friendship has to go beyond "I'll give 50 percent, but I expect 50 percent back." That's a good way to destroy a friendship—or a marriage, for that matter. One of the many problems in that attitude is our usual bad math—we figure we've given half when, at best, it may have been only ten percent.

Human friendship ought to be like God's friendship for us—"anyhow." We're friends, *anyhow*, no matter what. We can't ignore the faults of our friends, but we can be friends despite those little shortcomings. We give our friendship *unconditionally*, not with any fine print that says, "I'll be your friend *if* you change this or that in your personality" (which usually means "if you become more like me"). All of the above may help to explain why one's really close friends are very few and so precious.

Maybe the toughest thing to handle in a friendship (and yet it does usually crop up at one time or other) is the feeling that a trusted friend has let you down. Then you have to talk, certainly not clam up and brood. With honest talk, the misunderstanding will either convert back to understanding, or you'll have to admit that you didn't really have a good friend there in the first place. So you scratch one illusion and move ahead.

You might say that a true friend "sees the man within the monster." Dr. Frankenstein's monster once wandered into the cottage of a blind hermit, who judged him by his personhood, not by appearance. So the blind man accepted the monster as a friend. That's what real friends always do—befriend a person, not an appearance.

Years back, there was a great movie, *The Enchanted Cottage.* A man whose face had been badly disfigured in a war married a very homely girl. They were ashamed to let anyone else see them, so they always stayed home together. One day, though, they looked at each other and suddenly saw only beauty, with no trace of ugliness. They threw a big party, so everyone else could see this marvelous transformation. But as the couple came arm in arm down the stairs, the guests turned away in pity, seeing only ugliness.

Real friends see the beauty of the persons who are their friends, an inner beauty that, for them, beautifies and transforms the whole person. And Christians see beauty in their friends because they see Christ there!

So...?

So friends are great. Also necessary. In fact, friendship is one of the great Christian virtues—if we only "baptize" it properly. First we baptize it by our motivation—seeing Christ in others, no matter what they look like on the outside, or even how they sometimes act. We baptize it, too, by offering our friendship (starting with being "friendly") to everyone—not just the exteriorly attractive, not just those who like us or those we already like, not just the "greats," but everyone.

"...whatever you did for one of the least of these brothers of mine, you did for me." The Lord couldn't have made it any clearer than that!

15

"Love" vs. *Real* Love

Showtime!

Jennifer had bugged her parents so much about getting a dog that finally, on her twelfth birthday, they gave in and bought her an eight-week-old German shepherd puppy. "But," they warned her, "this dog is your responsibility. You feed her, take care of her, everything."

That didn't turn out to be any problem for Jennifer. Right away, she fell in love with Sam, as she named the puppy, thinking Sam a neat name for a little girl dog. Jennifer's responsibility was made a lot easier when it turned out that Sam was an exceptionally bright dog and would do anything to please Jennifer.

Besides being the greatest German shepherd ever created, in Jennifer's somewhat biased opinion, Sam was a comic, a showgirl. She soon caught on that she was supposed to pose whenever a camera showed up. And when she would "heel" next to Jennifer at an intersection, she would look around and grin at everyone to make sure she was noticed.

This show-business personality backfired once, however, the night of the obedience-school graduation. Since Sam learned quickly, she had done everything perfectly all through the three-month course. On graduation night, though, when the dogs were graded and given awards accordingly, she decided it was showtime, so she had a lot of fun hamming it up. That meant she lost all kinds of points and placed only fourth out of five dogs. Sam seemed to think that, since she knew all this stuff perfectly, this was the time to add a little color to it. So she enjoyed herself. But Jennifer did not.

To be fair to Sam, she did get gypped in one event. At "Down" and "Stay," she was the only dog of the five to obey right away, which meant she had to wait for three or four minutes for the others to get the idea. By the time they were all "down," she figured enough was enough, and since she didn't particularly care for her companions anyhow, she got up and rejoined Jennifer. Next, when Sam was "heeling" for the first time, she heard a rustle outside the fence about five yards away and figured she could check it out without breaking stride. Which she did fairly well, but the judges noticed. She did the "Come" after "Down" and "Stay" perfectly, but then instead of simply sitting quietly in front of Jennifer, she added a little flair and sat up. More points off. To cap the evening's performance, instead of simply going to Jennifer's left and sitting at the final "Heel," she went around behind Jennifer, stuck her head out from between the girl's legs, and grinned at the crowd—her audience, who thought it was pretty funny.

Jennifer was really down in the dumps over the whole thing, since she knew Sam could have easily walked away with first place. As time went on, though, she began to see the laughs in it, and the unimportance of getting a trophy when you could entertain others and have some fun yourself instead.

A few years later, when Jennifer was fifteen, she once

found herself way down in the dumps, discouraged mostly by her own mistakes. One night when she and Sam were alone in her room, she all but shouted at the Lord, "How can you possibly keep putting up with me?"

She didn't physically *hear* him answer, but he came though loud and clear anyhow: "You recall Sam's obedience school graduation, no?"

"Of course," Jennifer answered. *"That* I could never forget!"

"And," the Lord went on, "you will recall your disappointment at the time?"

"Sure. But I got over it. It was fun—well, later on, anyhow."

"Okay, so tell me—disappointed as you were then at her blowing it—did you ever stop loving Sam for a single moment later or even that night itself?"

"Of course not," Jennifer answered. There was no need for any further conversation. She got the point, and Sam grinned at her, apparently happy the girl had wised up. And brightened up.

Love *Lives* With Mistakes

Love doesn't deal with rating how perfect the loved one might be. Nor does love demand selfish changes. Nor does love lay down conditions like "I'll love you, Sam, *if* you come off with the first-place trophy."

Genuine Christian love is supposed to be like God's— overlooking faults, not demanding that the loved one change to suit the friend's image. Most of all, love is unconditional. Love is basically self-sacrificing, including when that sacrifice means a certain degree of apparent let-down or humiliation for oneself—for instance, when your friend stumbles or seems not to be as good as other people's friends. And sometimes love demands much bigger sacrifices. Like so. . . .

It was a rotten day, even by winter standards, as the 737

passed the point-of-no-return on D.C.'s frozen runway and tried to get airborne. Pilot and co-pilots struggled to get the icy-winged craft up, but it stalled, scraping the bridge over the Potomac, smashing several cars, then veering off to plunge into the ice-jammed river.

Seventy-eight people died.

During the bitter, frost-biting hours that followed, a helicopter team risked their lives, even dipping their skids into the icy river in their efforts to pull out the pitifully few survivors. Seeing an injured woman losing her struggle, a twenty-eight-year-old bystander jumped into the frigid water and dragged her ashore.

A middle-aged man no one was able to identify for some time was clinging to the broken craft's tailsection with five other survivors. Each time the helicopter team dropped a flotation ring, this man calmly handed it on to someone else. And when all the others had been lifted to safety and the chopper returned for this man, he was gone.

As *Time* magazine's Roger Rosenblatt put it:

> . . . nature cared nothing about the five passengers. Our man, on the other hand, cared totally. . . caring wholly on distinctions, principles, and, one supposes, faith. . . . If the man in the water gave a lifeline to the people gasping for survival, he was likewise giving a lifeline to those who observed him. . . . The man in the water pitted himself against an implacable enemy; he fought it with charity; and he held it to a standoff. He was the best we can do [1/25/82].

That man didn't lose, He won—big.

There's a classic picture, from the Special Olympics. A girl, winning her race, sees a nearby competitor stumble and fall to the track. With no hesitation, she goes back to help the fallen runner to her feet, while the others finish ahead of them both.

She didn't lose either. She won—big.

Call it anything you want—guts, humanity, instinct. But only one word sums it up exactly: *Christianity*. Oh, not the "Christianity" of the Pharisee, one who keeps most of the visible rules (at least the convenient ones) and looks down on others; or one who lives comfortably, declaring poverty and hunger "their own fault" and branding those who cry out about it as "bleeding-heart sociologists"; or one who sneers at the peacemakers as "unrealistic." No, not *that* "Christianity," but the real thing, the Christianity that *lives* Christ, that brings him and his full teaching and his love to our world. *That* Christianity.

And *that* Christianity and genuine love are the same thing.

Phony "Love"

Someone whose whole idea of love has come from pop songs and TV and such is probably identifying love with sex, and sex with "let's get physical." Both of these are major bloopers conceived *by* the mindless in search of a quick buck *for* the mindless ("the blind leading the blind") in search of a cheap thrill.

TV and other media immortals are forever latching on to terms that unfortunately are popularized for them by those who get their entire education, vocabulary included, from the boob tube. Only the very immature (no matter what their age) could take up unquestioningly such an expression as "having sex," or, worst of all, "making love." Nobody, but nobody, can *make* "love" happen, least of all by sexual activity, which is meant to be the result and culmination and completion, not just of physical attraction, but of a very special kind of bond between a husband and wife.

Among the other weird results of trying to make sex and love amount to the same thing is that it rules out most *kinds* of love: the right kind of self-love and the love of parents, of children, of friends, of strangers, and of those others Christ told us to love—our "enemies." The trouble is, we've been had. Without all the silly propaganda spread around about "love," we'd *know* right away what it really is, without having to cut through all the heaps of guck to find it.

Real Love

There was this group of psychologists who studied the inhabitants of a remote Mexican village. Among other questions the doctors asked was "What is love?" And these people (young and not so young), unspoiled by the junk our Western culture has been scattering around, came right to the heart of the matter. Like this one:

> "There are many kinds of love, for a plant, for the land. First, there is love of God . . . love of parents, of sweethearts, love of a husband or wife, love of children, love of a good friendship; even to raise an animal one must love. . . . The love of friends one retains even when they are away. . . . Love is a force that makes a person seek the well-being of those he esteems."

Before we got "educated," we knew that love, *real* love seeks primarily the good of another, and that the mere pur-

suit of our own jollies through another is not love at all
(although, of course, the self-seeker does like to call it that).
Love means, rather, "I think so much of you that I'm willing
to knock myself out for your own good, which may not
always be all that pleasant for me. I'm willing to sacrifice
'me,' and that includes my feelings, for your sake." So the
very first thing we have to learn, though it's more like re-
learn, about love is that it's genuine only when it goes out of
ourselves to others. Like Marian, in *Music Man*, sang about
her ideal man, "I would like him to be more interested in me
than he is in himself, and more interested in us than in me."
And vice versa, Marian!

Christian Love

Okay, so those are some accurate, if general, ideas about
genuine love. They describe loving as a human being, as a
maturing or mature person—not like some still self-centered
infant whose only way of telling good from bad, right from
wrong, love from non-love, is "Will it give me pleasure or
will it hurt?"

But we have to go even further than this, because we're
Christians. We claim to be followers of Jesus Christ, not only
in words and not just on Sundays (although we need that day
to make the other days work right), but in *all* our actions,
every day, every moment.

You get a hint of what real Christian love should be from
the very fact that you exist. God wouldn't have created us if
he didn't love unselfishly, not asking "What's in it for me?"
but motivated only by "What can I do for *them*?" Since God
is Love and shares his power to love with us, real love starts
with *unselfishness*. Lots of people have loved like this, asking only, "How can I help and protect this person?" Though
they are not publicity seekers, these people occasionally grab
our attention, as did Nobel Peace Prizewinner Mother Teresa
of Calcutta.

Christian love goes still further, like being willing to love someone even when it seems to be one-way, when the other person doesn't seem to return that love. That's a tough one, but if you think *that's* rough, wait till you hit the situation—as you almost certainly will—where someone apparently *stops* loving you!

At Tom Cassidy's funeral (check back to chapter 6), his friend Walter O'Keefe startled everyone during his eulogy by saying that "Tom loved like a dog." But the truth is that *God* loves that way—*unconditionally*, no matter what—and the genuine Christian must love the same way.

But Christian love goes further still: The Lord laid it right on the line. He told us to love our friends, sure, but also to love our enemies. Maybe you don't have any real "enemies." But there are possibly some near relatives of same who come close to qualifying. Like those you don't seem to like as well as you like others; those you don't know very well; "strangers"; those who seem boring or don't seem to warm up to anyone; and maybe, above all, those who have hurt you and who need your forgiveness. Or maybe the other way round—those whose forgiveness *you* need. And if you're a real Christian, that latter bit may mean seeking forgiveness even when you're afraid you may just get turned away.

The Lord summed it up in his parable of the Good Samaritan (Luke 10:30–37), a story he told in answer to this question: "Who *is* my neighbor, this character I'm supposed to love like myself?" You've read or heard the story often enough, so just recall a few important details of it here:

1. To the Jews, a Samaritan was a nothing or worse. And yet Christ makes a Samaritan the hero of the story, certainly to let them know that while "neighbor" in the Old Testament meant just "your own people," it now was to mean *everyone*.

2. This Samaritan didn't merely stop and do whatever he could on the spot; he interrupted his own important trip

and schedule to bring the injured man to a place he could be better cared for.

3. He didn't stick around to get repaid or even thanked.
4. He left money and his credit card to take care of anything else the injured man might need.

That's Christian love—the Good Samaritan, the man in the icy Potomac—the genuine Christian.

The apostle Paul did a pretty fair job of describing real love:

> Love is patient, love is kind. It does not envy, it does not boast, it is not proud. It is never rude, it is not self-seeking, it is not easily angered, it keeps no record of wrongs. Love does not delight in evil but rejoices with the truth. It always protects, always trusts, always hopes, always perseveres. Love never fails. . . (1 Cor. 13:4–8).

And why did Paul come up with that description of love? Because Christ's love is all those things. And our love had better be, too, if we're going to keep on calling ourselves "Christians."

16

Choosing to Reach Out

JOIN THE TOTALLY WALL-TO-WALL SUMMER PARTY

TWO SUN-PACKED MONTHS OF FUN AND GAMES, MAZATLAN, MEXICO

CRUISE DOWN ON THE *QUEEN HARRY*, RETURN ON *AERONAVES*

SHIPBOARD ROMANCES, SOUVENIRS

SWIM AND SURF ON BIKINI BEACHES

No ID NEEDED FOR MEXICAN BEER

FULL TWO MONTHS: HOTEL (DOUBLE OCCUPANCY), ROUND TRIP FARE: $750; ONE MONTH: $650; ONE DAY: $500

GET YOUR GANG TOGETHER AND REALLY *LIVE* FOR A SUMMER

---

600 ORPHANS AND CHRIST NEED YOU THIS SUMMER AT CUERNA-VACA, MEXICO: *Nuestros pequeños hermanos y hermanas* (our little brothers and sisters) HIS TWO FAVORITES BOTH IN ONE: POOR AND KIDS

COME AND BUILD A SCHOOL, DIG A DITCH, PAINT A HOUSE, FEED A CHILD, TEACH, WHATEVER

PREPARE IN "BOOT CAMP" TWO WEEKS . . . LEARNING YOUR "JOB," MEETING YOUR TEAM-MATES, HOW TO LIVE IN TENTS AND ON CHUCKWAGON MEALS

WE GO AND RETURN BY BUS

YOU PAY, BUT YOU CAN MAKE IT ON $25 A MONTH . . . A SUMMER IS A TERRIBLE THING TO WASTE!

Heaped-Up Treasure?
Or Gone with the Wind?

Check out these ads from the final issue of the school year for *Hyper-High Lights.*

Most of the kids at Hyper High only sighed over the ads knowing they would have to stay home all summer and earn some cash. Others just weren't interested—they had enough plans for fantastic operations out of their home base.

Tom and his twin sister Kate decided to try the Mazatlan deal. Their parents were loaded, and so were all their friends' folks, including their classmate Brenda's. But when Brenda told her friend Frank she was going to try for the orphanage trip, he decided on that, too. He might have liked to do Mazatlan, but he wasn't sure he could hack the money part of it. Besides, he liked being near Brenda, and she didn't seem to mind having him around.

During the first days of the new school year that September, everybody was talking about the past summer. Tom and Kate were especially high on the ball they had had at Mazatlan, all the great kids they met, all the beer they knocked off, the neat souvenirs they brought back. Brenda and Frank didn't have much to say when Tom and Kate were reliving their fun-filled summer for the crowd. "Digging a few ditches" and "building a barn" just didn't seem to compare.

As the school year went on, of course, memories of summer faded. There were more important things to plan now. Kate and Tom were already on committees for prom planning, preparing from a distance by lots of party practice. Frank and Brenda were wondering occasionally how they might be able to get back to Cuernavaca. Sometimes they asked each other if Mazatlan might not be better next time, more fun anyhow. Now and then, though, a letter or postcard would come to one of them, sometimes in Spanish, sometimes so badly scrawled they could hardly de-code it. But every letter carried the same message: "Many *graciases* for all you did for us last summer. We will never forget you. Mostly you showed us that *los Americanos de los Estados Unidos del Norte* are *magnificos Christianos*, even though your *periodicos* never show you like that. We love you."

So Frank and Brenda made the same choice the next summer, Cuernavaca. After all, they realized, once the Mazatlans are over, all you have left are memories, not all of them great. But after even a short time with "*nuestros pequeños hermanos y hermanas*," you had something a lot more visible. And valuable. And permanent. . . .

There are lots and lots of Toms and Kates, who symbolize people living mostly for themselves and only for the moment. But there are also a surprising number of Brendas and Franks, who live with purpose, for something more valuable and lasting as they reach out to others.

Christian Choices = Mature Choices

In this part of the book, we're into *living* as Christians instead of only talking about it. Now—keeping in mind what we know of *Christian* friendship and love—let's think about the way we maturing Christians ought to be making our choices.

As time goes on, the choices and decisions in your life become less your parents' and more your own. If those choices are to be truly and more exclusively yours, you'll have to have the maturity to make them on the right basis. That will mean making them as a Christian.

One of the top shrinks in the educational field has spent a lot of his professional life trying to figure out what he calls "stages of maturity." He keeps changing the specifics, but he's generally decided that a human being goes *from* (1) emphasizing respect for (even fear of) authority, *to* (2) developing one's own mind and will, to (3) a slight but growing awareness of one's responsibility to others, and finally to (4) the realization of one's responsibility for a thing known as "the common good."

There may not seem to be anything exactly "Christian" about that process, but there really is. With a little adjustment, you can come up with a Christian parallel in maybe five stages: 1. Emphasizing one's feelings as guides, but moving toward convictions, faith-convictions included; 2. a growing sense of a true scale of values; 3. the awareness of others as made in the image of God, like oneself, and thus a brothers-and-sisters relationship; 4. an awakening to what is meant by sharing and serving (as we Christians are billed as doing); 5. the realization that true joy and happiness can't be latched on to in any other way—here or later.

You can see that all those theoretical stages involve choices. So we prove or disprove both our maturity and our Christianity by the way we choose. The totally immature, no matter what their age, will make their choices with only themselves in mind. And they won't look too far ahead, their main question being "What's in it for me, here and now?"

But if we're maturing on schedule, our choices will increasingly be taking into account our responsibility to others and what effect our choices will have on them. We'll also be looking down the line a bit, wondering what effect each choice is going to have over the long haul.

So we "baptize," or Christianize, our maturity mainly by our motive: Christ told us to choose with these things in mind. Each choice you make will have an effect on you, both now and in your future. But it will also have an effect, no matter how seemingly slight or even invisible, on the whole human race. You either uplift the human race or degrade it— largely by your choices. Are they the choices of Christian, or not?

But let's leave the theories and get down to some cases. . . .

You're making choices every day—concerning yourself, your friends and others you encounter, your parents, your home and neighborhood, your school and church, all your activities. You make those choices with either an attitude of "What will it do for me?" or "What will it do for others?" And that latter attitude means simply considering what, as a maturing person and as a Christian, you should decide. Maybe the easiest way to think this out would be to compare some immature choices with the maturing Christian one:

Immature	Mature—Christian
"Lois is boring. I avoid her."	"Lois may be lonely. I'll go out of my way to see if I can help."
"Joe wants to go to a movie, but I want to go to the dance, so we dance."	"I'd sooner go to the dance, but my friend Joe wants to see that movie, and he let me choose last time."
"I'm going to really enjoy this date with Janet."	"I'm going to make sure Janet really enjoys our date."
"Fred asked me to the prom, but I'll wait to see if Gomer asks."	"I'd sooner go to the prom with Gomer, but Fred asked me first, so I'm going with him."
"I'd better get my money's worth out of this date."	"Lord, help us both to get to know each other on this date tonight."
"What do I get?"	"What can I give?"
"I'll just claim 'schoolwork' until the dishes are done."	"I'll do my share—just as Christ helped out in that carpentry shop."

"I'd sooner phone Gladys than do that schoolwork."

"I'll get my schoolwork done first—maybe I'll learn something."

"I'm going to watch *I was a 120-Pound Teen Scorpion* on TV."

"I'll get a lot more out of doing my Bible-study preparation than from the junk on TV tonight."

"Talk about a 'generation gap'—my parents really turn me off!"

"I guess a guy's parents are his friends, too. And maybe that 'generation gap' is partly *my* fault."

"My parents don't understand. I'd like to trade them in for someone who'd care what happens to me."

"Without my parents I wouldn't be here, or have survived, or even have a home. That makes them sound a lot like God!"

"That's sure a Do-Good pious bunch involved in the school's food-basket for-the-poor projects."

"I'll risk being called a Do-Gooder if I can help some of the poor and hungry."

"If I go up to the orphanage to help out, I'll miss all the Saturday morning pep rallies."

"I like the idea of 'being' Christ for a bunch of lonely orphans."

"My friends will laugh at me if I go to church when they don't."

"I get some of the ammo for being a Christian at church, so that makes going regularly a lot more important than what anybody might say about me."

"I'll take Phys Ed instead of math. It's easier."

"Math may be something I'll need, so I'll take it even though it's tough."

"I'll carry the condoms they gave out at school, just in case, or maybe even as a hint."

"Mary isn't speaking to me, so I'll show her—I'll make sure she knows I'm snubbing her."

"Christ never said that 'legal' and 'moral' are the same. Like if somebody gave you a gun, it wouldn't make it right to shoot somebody."

"Mary isn't speaking to me, but the Lord said to love your enemies. So I'll bowl her over with my own cheery greetings, no matter how *she* acts."

Mature choices are unselfish choices.

Banking It—Or Blowing It

Okay, so those are a few of the choices you have to make every day. There are those bigger choices down the road, too, like what you're going to do with the rest of your life. Again, this is a choice, and it's yours. But let's hope it will be one made not just to please yourself, but one that will somehow or other have some worthwhile effect on everybody you meet in your life—and even on all those you never directly encounter! Of all the choices you make, your choice of a state of life, your "vocation" if you will, is the most important decision for yourself and for the world. You sure don't want your life to be like that of the hippie we noticed in chapter 8: "He Lived. He Died. Groovy." And that was it.

In however quiet a way, you want to have some positive, Christian influence on your world. Maybe your choice will be directly connected with bringing Christ to others, full time. Maybe your choice will mean bringing him to others through some other profession you will have chosen. Maybe it will mean preaching. Maybe it will mean not just "How can I make the most money?" but "How can I use my profession and whatever else I have to be a real Christian, and so to *be* Christ for others?" Whatever your choice of a profession and lifestyle and such, if you're really a Christian, you will be committed to bringing the Lord to others through your own personality and with your own talents and circumstances. Like this, from *A Pocketful of Prayers*:

> The bricklayer laid a brick on the bed of cement. Then, with a precise stroke of his trowel, spread another layer. And laid on another brick. The foundation grew visibly, the building rose, tall and strong, to shelter people. I thought, Lord, of that poor brick in the darkness at the base of the big building. No one sees it, but it accomplishes its task, and the other bricks need it. Lord, what difference whether I am on the rooftop or in the foundations of your building, as long as I stand faithfully at the right place?

Be a brick!

17

Frosting? Or the Whole Cake?

Terry's Legacy

Nobody was sure when Terry had come to Denver. She was just there. Nor was anybody able to find out where she had come from, this lovely girl of about nineteen, beautiful and full of life.

Terry painted portraits and, she said, had been supporting herself through them for about four years. Denver people soon discovered her, and her portraits drew some big commissions, some, in fact, out of sight. Suddenly, though, she decided to give up portrait painting because, with her uncompromising honesty, she said, "I feel like a hypocrite painting people the flattering way they wish they were. I'd sooner bring out some of what's inside."

So she began to do mostly landscapes and abstracts. Once again, though, her honesty got in the way, and she refused to sell some of her paintings to people she said "who don't understand what it's all about." Even when she was offered huge sums for some of them, she would refuse to sell if the buyer didn't seem to understand. On the other hand, sometimes she'd give a valuable painting away to someone who *did* understand!

Terry lived alone in her studio apartment. During the Denver winters, the neighbors would sometimes see her out playing in the snow with the little kids. Clearly, the little people accepted her without question as one of them, only bigger. She would show them how to make snow tunnels and forts, and roll and wrestle with them, having a ball.

Somehow or other, when someone was ill in the neighborhood, Terry would show up to see if she could be of any help. She seemed to have radar for finding the lonely and spending some time with them. Even strangers on the street always got a big hello from her.

Terry had one little peculiarity. Well, of course there were those who thought everything about her was "peculiar." Like the town bigots who started rumors when they noticed that not all of her friends, kids and non-kids, were lily-white. When Terry was walking somewhere and not in any big hurry, she would go up to a door, knock, and greet whoever answered with "Would you like to talk about Jesus for a while?"

Now that could be quite startling, but nobody ever turned her off once they recovered from the opening shock. She'd startle them again when she began the conversation with "Do you know that you *are* Jesus Christ?" But then she'd go on to explain that those of us who claim to be Christians either bring Jesus to others in our own personalities and in our way of living and our example, or else we're not Christians at all, only phonies.

And, of course, she was right.

Terry was bubblingly enthusiastic about her faith in Jesus

and proud of it. So she never tried to hide it. On the contrary! She pulled off one of her most memorable bits of evidence for this one evening when she decided she'd like to spend some time in prayer in a nearby church. But when she got to the church she found it locked. That burned her, so she was soon pounding on the pastor's door, then loudly and angrily proclaiming to him, and to the neighborhood, "Don't you dare try to lock the Lord away from me!"

Terry vanished from the city as abruptly and mysteriously as she had arrived, with nobody noticing at the time. Her destination, like her origin, was unknown. But no one who ever met her would ever be able to forget her. That pastor especially wished she were still around, because she'd taught him something—and she'd given the city something unforgettable. And very, very important.

The Christ-Bearer

Okay, so we're not all Terrys. In fact, no one else is Terry but Terry, just as no one is you but you. So not all of us, or even many of us, can bring Christ to others exactly the way she did. But you can bring Christ to others *your* way, the way only you can. As someone has remarked, "*You* may be the only Bible someone may ever read."

You may have seen a medal of St. Christopher, the patron saint of travelers, in someone's car, or at least have heard of him. (Some say he relinquishes his protection and jumps out of the car, however, when it gets very much over the speed limit!) His name, which means "Christ-bearer," is your name, too. You carry Christ to others, in your own unique way, with your own degree of strength.

This responsibility will mean *living* as a Christian—not just talking a great game of Christianity; not just going to church now and then; not merely tossing off an occasional prayer; not just carrying an ID card marked "Christian." No, you either live daily as a Christian, or you're not one.

"Being" Christ

For all too many card-carrying Christians, their professed faith means only certain kinds of things: going to church sometimes, especially at Christmas and Easter, and contributing to the collection; living a reasonably clean life, without overdoing it; praying now and then, especially when in a corner. Those "Christians" are apt to associate only with their own clones, who think and act just the way they do and preferably look like them too. This is not unlike the Pharisees of Christ's historical day and of our own day as well, who considered anyone (like Samaritans or the disabled) not resembling themselves as a sinner.

Christianity is not occasional piety or a once-in-a while good deed. It's a way of living, and if you don't live that way, you're not a Christian. It's that simple.

You're not a Christian just in church or when kneeling in prayer. You're a Christian when you work or study or party or date, when you talk or play football or tennis or dance, when you're outrageously joyous or down in the dumps, when you feel just great or when you hurt. In all you do.

Christianity isn't something you slip into after all the day's or week's activities have been taken care of. It's not the frosting on the cake, but the cake itself! You can gather some of the ingredients for that cake in church and at prayer. But the ingredients are not Christianity until combined with love and worked, over a period of time, into one grand masterpiece.

Because most of us probably waste a lot of time imagining a future where we will be heroic Christians, we let the present slip by. And when we try to outline what it means to be a Christian, we may sometimes think only of those noble moments when we can shine. Make no mistake about it—an occasion may well come sometime in your life when choosing some degree of "heroism" may be the only way to demonstrate some element of your Christianity. But that's not the ordinary, continuous lifestyle of the garden-variety Christian. The basic, consistent Christian qualities are very ordinary-seeming human traits. All we need do to make them *Christian* qualities, or virtues, is "baptize" them.

We baptize them in two ways: (1) by our motive (*seeing* Christ in others and *being* Christ for others), and (2) by "universalizing" them (for example, being kind, not just to those we naturally like, but to everyone—friend, stranger, "enemy," the works).

So let's take a look at a few of those "ordinary" qualities. . . .

Friendliness

There's no such thing as an unfriendly Christian. How could there be when all Christians are told to love even their "enemies"?

Notice, though, it's friend-*liness*, not friend-*ship* that we're talking about. Everybody, Christian, pagan, or whatever, is usually nice to friends. In fact, God's Old Testament mandate to "love your neighbor as yourself" followed this: "Do not seek revenge or bear a grudge against one of your people" (Lev. 19:18). Jesus "Christianized" that commandment:

> "You have heard that it was said, 'Love your neighbor and hate your enemy.' But I tell you; Love your enemies and pray for those who persecute you. . . . If you love those who love you, what reward will you get? . . . And if you greet only your brothers, what are you doing more than others? Do not even pagans do that?" (Matt. 5:43–47).

To make it still clearer, he followed it up with that Good Samaritan story, whose hero came from a race hated by that period's crop of bigots, the spiritual ancestors of today's racists.

We baptize—"Christianize"—that natural virtue of friendliness, then, by being friendly with everyone, not so they'll consider us great people, but because we're trying to bring Christ to them. We treat them as we would Christ himself. If we're friendly with Christ, we have to live that spirit of friendliness, by being friendly toward everyone: strangers, those of other races or religions or even those with no visible religion at all. (And if we are "unfriendly," there's little hope of nudging the latter type into even remotely thinking about "getting religion.") That friendliness will also extend to those people who are paid to serve you—waiters, gas-pumpers, salesclerks—and those you are paid to serve, even when *they* come on as slavemasters.

Kindness, Thoughtfulness

It shouldn't take any persuasion to realize that a Christian must be kind (as Christ was and is) and, hopefully, thoughtful. The difference between those two qualities is that thoughtfulness takes up where kindness left off. It's "kind" to give your mother a present on Mothers' Day; it's thoughtful, though risking the severe shock she may experience, to push her out of the kitchen and do the dishes unforced on some ordinary weeknight.

Kindness, of course, has a lot of outlets, like reaching out to others or readily forgiving them when necessary. Like Christ. Did you ever notice, by the way, that Jesus never refused to forgive those who asked and never bawled them out? But he did bawl out, in no uncertain terms and some strong language, the snobs who criticized and looked down on those they labeled "sinners." And you'll notice that all his miracles were acts of kindness, no matter what other motive might also have been there.

We reach out in our kindness to everyone, not to be thought of as a neat person, but because Christ said, "What you do to them, you do to me." And so, in our personal brand of kindness, we bring Christ and his kindness to them.

Compassion

"Compassion" means "suffering with," so it goes beyond sensitivity. You can be sensitive to someone else's suffering or problem and still carefully avoid having to share in it, even mentally. Sometimes we even act on this attitude semi-piously, thanking the Lord that we're not hungry, but giving little thought, and even less action, to those who are. The compassionate person will somehow convey, though not necessarily by words, that he understands *and* somehow shares in another's pain, wishing he could help in some way and doing just that when he can.

Only one totally compassionate person has ever lived: Jesus Christ, who suffered and died for all of us. That little word *for* has two meanings: "in our place" and "on our behalf." That makes his suffering and dying for us perfect and total compassion, a degree of compassion none of us can reach, but a virtue all of us can imitate, each in his own unique, limited way. Our compassion, if Christian, reaches out to everyone, as we try to bring them Christ through our Christian living.

The Right Kind of Pride

The Christian can't be pressured into backing down from his or her Christian principles by the threat of possible ridicule—like "Hey, you don't really believe that extramarital sex is wrong, do you? Today? What a nerd!" Or "Abortion's legal, so it must be okay. So how come *you* don't seem to dig that? You retarded or something?" No, there's a real pride in being a Christian, and that goes along with pride in being your own person. It's a pride, for example, in being devoted to your faith and its practice, even when some of your peers seemingly give up on it and maybe wonder (or so you imagine) how come you are so out of things as to keep at it.

Notice, this is not a pride in yourself but in the gifts the

Lord has given you in your faith. You're so proud of your faith that you won't consider weakening or abusing it. And just as you Christianize all these natural qualities by relating them to everyone, so you baptize this pride by extending it— and your kindness and all else—to everyone of all faiths.

Joy and Enthusiasm

If we are really living this Good News, our joy and enthusiasm will, like Terry's, be contagious and will probably cause the unbeliever to wonder, "What *is* it that makes this character so happy?" So those who see your joy and enthusiasm may just check out "that Christianity thing," without the formality of a teaching sermon. Many a heart has been opened to the gospel message by seeing a real Christian who obviously glories in his or her faith.

Like the other qualities, we show this joy and enthusiasm to everyone we encounter—parents, peers, teachers, checkout clerks, and order takers at Burger King. And, of course, our "enemies."

So...?

If it's truly Christian, our joy and enthusiasm won't be destroyed by occasionally rotten feelings, because our conviction of faith will be rock solid. Our basic reasons for joy (sometimes despite our feelings) will stay with us, because we will *know* that even life's difficulties and pain are valuable to us as Christian persons, now *and* down the road—all the way down the road. The Good News makes the whole bundle good, and so a cause for joy. Tom Cassidy, whom you've already met in chapters 6 and 15, once wrote this, after experiencing the Lord's forgiveness:

And so we move on . . . with the faces of our souls washed, as would a mother for a soiled child . . . and the sun breaks through, and the horizon looks, once more, absolutely attainable, and we skip and we hop and we hum, whistle or sing, and kick the leaves on the road with our happy toes.

Now *that's* the Christian!

All our lives, we seem to be graduating *from* something or other. When we're young, it's a school we leave behind—you even see little kindergarten kids in caps and gowns (cute stuff). When we're older, we "graduate" *from* being financially dependent on our parents, *from* the single state, usually, and *from* one or another stage in a career. All those imply an ending of sorts.

But mostly, graduation marks a step *to* a new beginning. As you graduate *from* something like junior or senior high or college, you may breathe a sigh of relief. Of course. It's nice to have that much over with, at least some parts of it. But now you move on. . . .

You will leave the stage and footlights of your graduation ceremony with a somewhat heady feeling. But don't confuse the excitement of the congratulations and applause with continuing reality. A graduate steps out of the lights and off the stage *into* the real world—*into* what life brings and what can be made of it. You have a few of the tools, and you'll discover that you need a lot more as you go. You will continue to collect those tools as your life unfolds. But the important thing is to use them!

"In the shadow of your wings, O Lord, I shout for joy!"